THE AGE OF
MAGICAL
OVERTHINKING

THE AGE OF MAGICAL OVERTHINKING

Notes on Modern Irrationality

Amanda Montell

Thorsons
An imprint of HarperCollins*Publishers*
1 London Bridge Street
London SE1 9GF
www.harpercollins.co.uk

HarperCollins*Publishers*
Macken House, 39/40 Mayor Street Upper
Dublin 1, D01 C9W8, Ireland

First published in the US by One Signal Publishers/Atria Books,
an imprint of Simon & Schuster, LLC 2024
First published in the UK by Thorsons 2024
This edition published 2026

1 3 5 7 9 10 8 6 4 2

© Amanda Montell 2024

Amanda Montell asserts the moral right to be
identified as the author of this work

Interior design by Timothy Shaner,
NightandDayDesign.biz

A catalogue record of this book is
available from the British Library

ISBN 978-0-00-870115-4

Printed and bound in the UK using 100% renewable
electricity at CPI Group (UK) Ltd

All rights reserved. No part of this publication may be reproduced,
stored in a retrieval system, or transmitted, in any form or by any means,
electronic, mechanical, photocopying, recording or otherwise,
without the prior written permission of the publishers.

Without limiting the exclusive rights of any author, contributor or the publisher
of this publication, any unauthorised use of this publication to train generative artificial
intelligence (AI) technologies is expressly prohibited. HarperCollins also exercise their
rights under Article 4(3) of the Digital Single Market Directive 2019/790 and
expressly reserve this publication from the text and data mining exception.

For Casey

Author's Note

Real events and characters from my life are described according to the best of my memory. Some names and identifying details have been changed.

Contents

Make It Make Sense
An intro to magical overthinking
1

1.

Are You My Mother, Taylor Swift?
A note on the halo effect
9

2.

I Swear I Manifested This
A note on proportionality bias
29

3.

A Toxic Relationship Is Just a Cult of One
A note on the sunk cost fallacy
52

4.

The Shit-Talking Hypothesis
A note on zero-sum bias
70

5.
What It's Like to Die Online
A note on survivorship bias
90

6.
Time to Spiral
A note on the recency illusion
107

7.
The Scammer Within
A note on overconfidence bias
129

8.
Haters Are My Motivators
A note on the illusory truth effect
151

9.
Sorry I'm Late, Must Be Mercury in Retrograde
A note on confirmation bias
169

10.
Nostalgia Porn
A note on declinism
185

11.
The Life-Changing Magic of Becoming a Mediocre Crafter
A note on the IKEA effect
203

Acknowledgments, 221

Notes, 225

Index, 245

The Age of Magical Overthinking

MAKE IT MAKE SENSE
An intro to magical overthinking

The attempts I made to get out of my own head were sundry and full of nonsense.

I visited a petting zoo for adults. I tried learning to meditate from a British computer voice. I stocked up on an unregulated nutrition powder called "Brain Dust." My brain felt like dust. In the last few years, "dread for no reason" became one of my most frequent Google searches, as if the act of typing my feelings to a robot would make them go away. I gorged myself on podcasts about women who'd "snapped," at once repulsed and tantalized by those who wore their madness on their sleeves. How good it must feel to "snap," I thought. My most cinematic attempt at mental rehab involved picking herbs on a farm in Sicily under a light-pollution-free sky. ("At night here, the stars are so close, they could fall into your mouth," the herb farmer told me, sending my heart to my throat.) With varying degrees of "success," I was doing everything I could think of to defect from the state of overwhelm and consumption that had become my life in the roaring 2020s. Anything to gain some perspective on the mental health exigency I'd been experiencing, and trying to rationalize, for the better part of a decade.

Every generation has its own brand of crisis. Those of the 1960s and '70s were about gaining freedom from physical tyrannies—equal rights and opportunities to vote, learn, work, mobilize. They were crises of the body. But as the century turned, so did our struggles inward. Paradoxically, the more collective progress we made, the more individual malaise we felt. Discourse about our mental unwellness crescendoed. In 2017, *Scientific American* declared that the nation's mental health had declined since the 1990s and that suicide rates were at a thirty-year high. Four years later, a CDC survey found that 42 percent of young people felt so sad or hopeless in the last two weeks that they couldn't go about their normal days. The National Alliance on Mental Illness in the US reported that between 2020 and 2021, crisis calls to their lifeline were up 251 percent. We're living in what they call the "Information Age," but life only seems to be making less sense. We're isolated, listless, burnt out on screens, cutting loved ones out like tumors in the spirit of "boundaries," failing to understand other people's choices or even our own. The machine is malfunctioning, and we're trying to think our way out of it. In 1961, Marxist philosopher Frantz Fanon wrote, "Each generation must, out of relative obscurity, discover its mission, fulfill it or betray it." Our mission, it seems, has to do with the mind.

My fixation with modern irrationality took root while I was writing a book about cults. It was 2020, and looking into the mechanics of cultlike influence during that year's existential imbroglio cast new light on the many faces of twenty-first-century derangement. Since the new millennium, humanity had built a megamall full of fun and fresh ways to dissociate: Fringe conspiracy theories had gone mainstream. Celebrity worship reached a hallucinatory zenith. Disney Adults and MAGA zealots were blackout drunk on nostalgia, drowned in chimeras of the past. These misbeliefs came in a range of flavors, from whimsical to warlike, but one thing was certain—our shared grasp on reality had slipped.

The only explanation for this mass head trip that made any sense to me had to do with *cognitive biases*:* self-deceptive thought patterns that developed due to our brains' imperfect abilities to process information from the world around us. Social scientists have described hundreds of cognitive biases over the last century, though "confirmation bias" and the "sunk cost fallacy" were the two that came up most in my reporting. Perusing just a few of these studies crystallized so much of the zeitgeist's general illogic, like people

---

* A term coined in 1972 by behavioral economists (and real-life besties) Amos Tversky and Daniel Kahneman.

with master's degrees basing their social calendars on Mercury's position in the cosmos, or our neighbors opting not to get vaccinated because a YouTuber in palazzo pants said it would "downgrade their DNA." Cognitive biases also explained scads of my own irrationalities, personal choices I could never justify to myself, like the commitment in my early twenties to stick out a romantic relationship that I knew caused me suffering, or my tendency to engineer online enemies based on conflicts I'd invented. I needed to yank at that thread. I had to understand how these mental magic tricks we play on ourselves combine with information overload like a chemistry experiment gone haywire—Mentos and Diet Coke.

Our minds have been fooling themselves since the dawn of human decision-making. The amount of input from the natural world alone was always too much for us to handle; cataloging the precise color and shape of every twig in order to understand it would take more than a lifetime. So, early brains came up with shortcuts that allowed us to make sense of our environment enough to survive it. The mind has never been perfectly rational, but rather *resource-rational*—aimed at reconciling our finite time, limited memory storage, and distinct craving for events to feel meaningful. Epochs later, the quantity of details to process and decisions to make has exploded like confetti, or shrapnel. We can't hope to mull over every datapoint as deeply as we might like. So we tend to rely on our ancestors' clever cheats, which come so naturally to us, we're almost never aware of them.

Faced with a sudden glut of information, cognitive biases cause the modern mind to overthink and underthink the wrong things. We obsess unproductively over the same paranoias (Why did Instagram suggest I follow my toxic ex-boss? Does the universe hate me?), but we blitz past complex deliberations that deserve more care. I have more than once experienced the disorientation of engaging in some battle of wits online, only to come up for air and feel in my body like I'd been using sparring tactics better suited to a Neolithic predator than a theoretical conversation. "I think because we have come so far technologically in the past 100 years, we think that everything is knowable. But that's both so arrogant and so fucking boring," said Jessica Grose, *New York Times* opinion columnist and author of *Screaming on the Inside: The Unsustainability of American Motherhood*, in 2023. I've been referring to this era, when we're so swiftly outpacing the psychological illusions that once served us, as the "Age of Magical Overthinking."

Broadly, magical thinking describes the belief that one's internal thoughts can affect external events. One of my first exposures to the concept came from Joan Didion's memoir *The Year of Magical Thinking*, which vivifies grief's power to make even the most self-aware minds deceive themselves. Mythologizing the world as an attempt to "make sense" of it is a unique and curious human habit. In moments of fierce uncertainty, from the sudden death of a spouse to a high-stakes election season, otherwise "reasonable" brains start to buckle. Whether it's the conviction that one can "manifest" their way out of financial hardship, thwart the apocalypse by learning to can their own peaches, stave off cancer with positive vibes, or transform an abusive relationship to a glorious one with hope alone, magical thinking works in service of restoring agency. While magical thinking is an age-old quirk, *over*thinking feels distinct to the modern era—a product of our innate superstitions clashing with information overload, mass loneliness, and a capitalistic pressure to "know" everything under the sun.

In 2014, bell hooks said, "The most basic activism we can have in our lives is to live consciously in a nation living in fantasies. . . . You will face reality, you will not delude yourself." To become as aware as we can of the mind's natural distortions, to see both the beauty and utter folly in them: This, I believe, ought to be part of our era's shared mission. We can let the cognitive dissonance bring us to our knees, or we can board the dizzying swing between logos and pathos. We can strap in for a lifelong ride. Learning to stomach a sense of irresolution might be the only way to survive this crisis. That's precisely what this exploration of cognitive biases has helped me do. Even more than Sicilian stargazing, writing this book has been the one thing that's kept the buzz in my head at a decibel level I can stand.

The Zen Buddhists have a word, "koan," which means "unsolvable riddle": You break the mind in order to reveal deeper truths and reassemble the pieces to create something new. I wrote this book as a yearning, a Rorschach test, a PSA, and a love letter to the mind. It's not a system of thought, but rather something more like a koan. If you have all but lost faith in others' ability to reason, or have made a cornucopia of questionable judgments that you can't even explain, my hope is for these chapters to make some sense of the senseless. To crack open a window in our minds, and let a warm breeze in. To help quiet the cacophony for a while, or even hear a melody in it.

ONE

ARE YOU MY MOTHER, TAYLOR SWIFT?
A note on the halo effect

The level of worship had gotten ravenous. Spiritually ravenous. Of course, people had always been overly worshipful—religion had forever been way too much, honor killings and all that—but now our gods weren't imaginary figments painted as all-knowing and faultless; they were mortal human celebrities, who we knew for sure were not. The new extremists were called "stans," a term originated by the rapper Eminem, whose 2000 song "Stan" spins a demented parable about a guy who blows a gasket after his icon won't answer his fan letters. Conspicuously, the word is also a perfect hybrid of "stalker" and "fan." The stans all had monastic names, like Barbz and Little Monsters and Beliebers and Swifties. They were said to be the death of dialogue. Critics stopped publishing negative reviews of pop stars' albums for fear of the mob—of getting "canceled" and "doxxed," of having their home addresses sleuthed and leaked and death threats sent. No one was leaving their couch, but everyone was afraid. No one was speaking out loud, but the world felt like one big shriek, an eight-billion-piece orchestra tuning and tuning ad infinitum. The stans were powerless as individuals. But as a flock, they'd "come for your neck," *Lord of the Flies*–style. Journalists feared for their necks—not war journalists, *music* journalists. The stans would cancel anyone, they'd even eat their own. They'd eat their very own god if it came to it. They'd eat their own god, especially. That's how ravenous things had gotten.

In 2023, a Taylor Swift devotee named Amy Long emailed me a three-thousand-word document breaking down all the pop star's major stan scandals from the past five years—emotional cataclysms, where Swifties turned against their exalted queen for failing to live up to qualities she never had and commitments she didn't make. The scandals, involving everything from ticket sales fiascos to rumors about her sexuality, bore dramatic titles in the style of Watergate: Ticketgate, Lavendergate, Jetgate, Moviegate, Tumblrgate. "This might be the most interesting," penned Long, creator of the Instagram account @taylorswift_as_books, in reference to the latter opprobrium: After years of casually interacting with fans on Tumblr, Swift permanently logged off the platform in 2020, feeling bulldozed by a throng of politically enraged obsessees. As Long explained it, stans got pissed after Swift posted a few tweets condemning Donald Trump and police brutality, but she never took her political vocalizations any further. From the stans' perspective, their idol had dangled a new era of progressive activism in front of them only to snatch it back, like a mother betraying a promise to her daughters. (Similar shouts of treason were echoed a few years later, when Swift started dating a sleazy edgelord from a pop-rock band. Stans wrote an "open letter" begging the star to dump their problematic new stepdaddy, swearing they wouldn't "step off his neck" until she did.)

Long went on: "A lot of fans have accused Taylor of using allyship as an aesthetic . . . and they get mad at her for not doing what they want . . . but she's a capitalist to her core. Most of her security team is ex–Special Forces, ex-FBI, or other former law enforcement officers. I'm not sure why fans expect her to be all, 'Defund the police! Tear down the system that made my dream come true.' . . . It's weird."

That thousands of strangers would morally lionize a famous singer based on conclusions about her character for which there was barely any evidence, then attempt to shake her off the pedestal with commensurate zeal after those assumptions wound up false, always seemed weird indeed. But the behavior is also explicable. I've come to attribute these increasingly common cycles of celebrity worship and dethronement—in addition to less parasocial love-hate dynamics with figures we know in real life—to a cognitive bias known as the *halo effect*.

Identified in the early twentieth century, the halo effect describes the unconscious tendency to make positive assumptions about a person's overall character based on our impressions of one single trait. We meet someone with a witty sense of humor and figure they must also be well-read and observant. Someone good-looking is presumed to be outgoing and confident. We think an artistic person is surely also sensitive and accepting. The term itself invokes the analogy of a halo, the power of good lighting alone to influence perceptions. Picture a twelfth-century religious painting: Commonly depicted wearing a crown of light, angels and saints are bathed in heavenly luster, a symbol of their overall goodness. Judging someone through the lens of the halo effect, our minds cast them in the same one-dimensionally warm glow, telling us to trust them wholesale, when they've objectively given us little reason to.

Behind the halo effect is a story of survival. Historically, aligning ourselves with a physically strong or attractive person proved a wise adaptive strategy, and it was generally fair to assume that one good quality indicated more. Twenty thousand years ago, if you encountered someone tall and muscular, you'd be reasonable to deduce they'd eaten more meat than average and were therefore likely a good hunter—someone you'd want in your corner. It was equally sensible to assume that a person with a symmetrical face and intact teeth had avoided disfigurement from lost battles and animal attacks, another decent role model. Today, singling out someone to look up to in life aids in identity formation, and when it comes to picking the right exemplar, we've learned to go with our gut. After all, how inefficient would it be to need all week to appraise a potential mentor, or to assemble a whole panel of perfectly qualified specialists—one for career insights, one for creative inspiration, another for fashion advice? To choose a sole role model for everything, based on hasty but overall sound generalizations, is simply a superior use of one's tight psychological budget. Voilà, the halo effect.

Parental figures were the bias's original subjects. Because our elders care for us and know things we don't, we figure they must know *everything*. Of my own mother, I believed this to an extreme. When it came to Dr. Denise Montell, the halo effect was inescapable. There was so much to live up to. A niche celebrity in her own right, my mother is a cancer cell biologist with a PhD from Stanford and a mantel full of awards for her research in molecular genetics. Last year, she was inducted into the National Academy of Sciences for discovering a mechanism of cell movement that could one day help cure cancer. My mother actually cured her *own* cancer. The week before I started sixth grade, when Denise was forty, she was diagnosed with a deadly lymphoma. I wouldn't learn until she'd been in remission for half a decade that the doctors had told her she was probably going to die. But she didn't die, in part because she collaborated with her oncologists to help design her own experimental treatment plan. Her research lab at Johns Hopkins was right across the street from the hospital where she'd squeeze in rounds of chemo on her lunch breaks. Now that course of treatment is standard practice for lymphoma patients all over the world.

As a child, most of my friends had single mothers and absentee dads. It's a peculiar coincidence, looking back. My friends' *Gilmore Girls*–style relationships with their moms—more intimate gal pals than the formal parent-offspring setup I knew—was no doubt part of what drew me to them in the first place. My friends' mothers were *so* human. They wore their imperfections on their sleeves. They had sailor mouths, sang off-key in the kitchen, and gave the silent treatment when they got angry. They spoke freely about period stains and bowel movements, body image and heartbreak. As a teenager, I found their vulnerability enamoring. Flaws weren't really Denise's style. No, not Denise, whose emotional cards were held close to the vest. Not Denise, whom I never saw make a single illogical mistake, who exercised for forty-five minutes every morning, never left the house without blowing out her chestnut hair to perfection, and who seemed to know everything in the universe, from how a single cell grows into a fetus to which bakery in town sold the tastiest French baguettes. My mother spent almost all of her time poring over her research at the lab downtown—late nights, every weekend—and her sangfroid combined with her absence rendered her almost mythical to me. I don't recall a time when I was not aware of her reputation, which dazzled like a platinum wedding band in the sun.

In theory, I wanted Denise to be rougher around the edges. I delighted in catching glimpses of it—like when she enjoyed half a margarita too many on a family vacation my junior year of high school and got all giggly as we jaunted back to the hotel room. Or when she'd tell me edgy anecdotes from her young adulthood, like the one where she almost got kidnapped the summer she lived in Paris at eighteen, or the college spring break when her surfer boyfriend convinced her to drop acid at a Grateful Dead concert. I loved imagining the person Denise was aside from my mother. But then, in practice, whenever she exhibited what I deemed an out-of-character emotion, even just losing her cool in traffic while running late to work, it appalled me. Her margin for error was so slim. She was the Taylor, I was the unhinged Swiftie. If Denise had a Tumblr, I definitely would've wanted her to like my posts and then bullied her off the platform the moment she wasn't the deity I built her up in my head to be.

But young people don't just look up to their moms anymore. In 2019, a Japanese study found that about 30 percent of adolescents aspire to emulate a media figure, like their favorite singer or athlete. A 2021 study published in the *North American Journal of Psychology* measured that celebrity worship had increased dramatically since two decades prior. The halo effect already makes it easy to deify someone you know in real life (as an adolescent, one of my unhealthiest social habits was engaging in lopsided friendships where I felt more like a fan than an equal, drawing false conclusions that because the popular girl in school had a bright smile and effortless charisma, she'd make a loyal confidante). It's even easier to engage in such infatuation from afar. Since we tend to view celebrities as attractive, wealthy, and successful, we snap-judge that they must also be sociable, self-aware, and worldly. Some admirers feel a deep closeness with their idols and figure their idols must cherish them, too, even maternally so. Not every fan is a stan, but celebrity worship is growing more extreme—and with measurable deleterious consequences.

The word "fan" stems from the Latin *fanaticus*, meaning "insanely but divinely inspired." It wasn't until the 1960s and '70s that the public started perceiving celebrities as anything more than entertainers, much less role models or gods. This shift in perception was connected to the rise in celebrity activism, which corresponded with Americans' loss of trust in politicians, traditional religious leaders, and healthcare authorities. In a *New York Times* op-ed titled "When Did We Start Taking Famous People Seriously?," Jessica Grose reported that in 1958, three quarters of Americans "trusted the federal government to do the right thing almost always or most of the time." That's according to Pew Research. But then the Vietnam War happened, and the economic recession of 1960, and (actual) Watergate, a tragic trifecta that suggested Americans needed to find a fresh kind of paragon. By the 1960s, baby boomers had become teenagers—there were more teens in the U.S. than ever—and as the isolation and insecurity that accompany adolescence coalesced with postwar prosperity and the itch of social change, young people found a new religion: the Beatles, whose members served not only as fans' artistic icons but distant lovers and spiritual guides.

In 1980, only about 25 percent of U.S. citizens trusted the government to do the right thing anymore. According to Grose, that's when the boundaries separating media figures, politicians, and spiritual authorities dissolved for good. In 1981, Ronald Reagan became America's first celebrity president, pitching himself as an "insurgent outsider." Hollywood's collective halo lit up like the burning bush, as the zeitgeist's new message implied that icons of the stage and screen weren't just here to entertain us, they were here to save us. Pop stars became our new priests. Eventually, social media fertilized that religiosity like potent manure. At my local crystal shop in L.A., you can find prayer candles printed with images of hallowed musicians: "Saint Dolly," "Saint Stevie," Harry Styles's face superimposed on the body of Christ. Grose quoted Dr. Paul Offit, a Children's Hospital of Philadelphia pediatrics professor and author of *Bad Advice: Or Why Celebrities, Politicians, and Activists Aren't Your Best Source of Health Information*, who analyzed that Americans put their faith in famous people because "we think we know them, we see them in movies or on TV and we assume they are the roles they play."

But celebrities also "play" themselves, and online, that show broadcasts 24/7. Even more disorienting than the Reagan era's Hollywood idolatry, when we see famous people air digital slices of their "real" personas, we feel like we know them wholly. Instagram captions appear like letters from a loved one; direct-to-cam posts seem like FaceTimes from a friend. In the age of magical oversharing, platforms like

Tumblr, TikTok, Instagram, and Patreon offer fans exponentially more access to personal information about their heroes, bridging the parasocial gap to make them feel ever more connected. After all, unlike TV, there is a real possibility that Taylor Swift could respond to your Instagram comment herself—the almighty saint answering her believer's prayer . . . or demand.

"If motivated enough, stans that congregate on social media actually can change the trajectory of their artist's path and the life of anyone who stands in the way," analyzed NPR music reporter Sidney Madden. "This shift in power dynamics . . . [creates] a feedback loop that can reward performative online personas more than genuine artistic vision."

Modern fandom falls on a spectrum, ranging from healthy admiration to pathological mania. The constructive end offers something transcendent. "Tumblr opened my eyes to scores of nuanced opinions from an array of people, in a space that wasn't intimidating to me," penned *Bustle* editor Danielle Colin-Thome in an essay on stan culture's "empowering—and at times, wildly problematic" role in the lives of marginalized youth. "Our fandoms . . . were vehicles to talk about larger issues—feminism, race, and LGBTQ representation." But the dogmatic end is no joke. A 2014 clinical examination of celebrity worship concluded that high levels of standom are associated with psychological difficulties, including "concerns about body image . . . greater proneness to cosmetic surgery, sensation-seeking, cognitive rigidity, identity diffusion, and poor interpersonal boundaries." Among other observed struggles were depression, anxiety, dissociation, narcissistic personality tendencies, thirst for fame, compulsive shopping and gambling, stalking behavior, excessive fantasizing to the point of social dysfunction (this was termed "maladaptive daydreaming"), addiction, and criminality. A 2005 study found that addiction and criminal activity were more strongly connected with celebrity worship than calcium intake with bone mass or lead exposure with children's IQs.

This 2005 study, published in the *Psychology, Crime & Law* journal, identified four categories along the celebrity worship continuum: First, there was the "Entertainment Social" level, defined by attitudes like, "My friends and I like to discuss what my favorite celebrity has done." Then, there was the "Intense Personal" feelings category, classified by statements like "I have frequent thoughts about my favorite celebrity, even when I don't want to." Third was the "Borderline-Pathological" level, characterized by delusional thoughts ("My favorite celebrity and I have our own code so we can communicate with each other secretly"); implausible expectations ("If I walked through the door of my favorite celebrity's home without an invitation, she or he would be happy to see me"); and self-sacrifice ("I would gladly die in order to save the life of my favorite celebrity"). A fourth category labeled "Deleterious Imitation" described stans willing to engage in licentious behaviors on behalf of their fave ("If I were lucky enough to meet my favorite celebrity, and s/he asked me to do something illegal as a favor, I would probably do it").

"She could push me pretty far, morally," said Jill Gutowitz, a pop culture reporter, author of the essay collection *Girls Can Kiss Now*, and unwavering Taylor Swift stan of ten years. Gutowitz has personally suffered at the hands of her fellow Swifties. She once found herself at the bottom of a vitriolic Twitter dogpile after penning a humorous review of Swift's *Lover* album for *Vulture*, in which she playfully poked fun at the singer's then boyfriend, actor Joe Alwyn, for being too bland to serve as her muse. ("Alwyn is a cup of plain oat milk," were Gutowitz's exact words.) "People got really mad at me for [that]," she reflected. "It was just one of those pile-on stan moments. I had an experience one time where the FBI knocked on my door because of something I tweeted, and still . . . I felt more scared when the Swifties came for me." But the mob was not enough to compromise Gutowitz's loyalty to the singer. Not even close. A few weeks of Twitter venom was par for the course, a nominal tax for the privilege of exalting Taylor Swift.

Precarious for both star and stan, the celebrity halo effect boasts the power to elevate a mortal being so high off the ground that the throng can't see their humanity anymore. By then, the worship itself becomes the subject, the celebrity something more like a mascot. In severe cases, the obsession grows so intense, a rat king of catharsis, that the wires between love and hate go scrambled. It's like that feeling of "cute aggression," where you squeeze a stuffed kitten so hard its head pops off. In 2023, after the chaotic rollout of Taylor Swift's live tour sales on Ticketmaster, stans erupted with charges of betrayal that went far beyond concert access. "People acted as though tickets were a human right Taylor denied them," Amy Long wrote in her email. "They kept moving the goalposts to the point that Taylor could only 'make up for it' by... giving them tickets, or playing acoustic sets at their houses.... [Taylor] is not someone who doesn't care about her fans, and it's as delusional to think that as it is to think she's actually your best friend."

Nearly every stan-worshipped A-lister has seen their flocks' mania pervert overnight from devotion to disdain. Even Beyoncé, who is exceptionally private, holding her admirers at a proscenium stage's length and mostly skirting tabloid controversy, has seen her disciples turn. The performer's ardent "BeyHive" supposedly lusted for any glimpse they could get into the life of their "flawless Queen"—that was, until she appeared on *Good Morning America* in 2015 to share the announcement that she'd gone vegan. Her stans thought she'd be "blessing" them with news of a pregnancy (a new "sibling"?) or live tour. When their expectations weren't met, they unleashed a deluge of relentless mockery, spamming the singer's social media comments with emojis of hamburgers and drumsticks.

Arguably, some of the decade's most venomous stan dynamics belong to English electropop artist Charli XCX. A particularly fervent corner of Charli's fan sect is occupied by white gay men, whose passion has been known to descend into bullying and objectification. Treating their diva as more of a prop than a person, "Charli's Angels" have coerced the singer into autographing and posing for photos with indecent objects including bottles of poppers, an anal douche, and a vial containing the ashes of one stan's deceased mother. They've viciously lambasted Top 40 hits of Charli's they didn't like, twisting her arm to alter her setlists on tour to meet their demands. I've seen tweets where Charli stans roasted her new releases as tragic "flops," then claimed her as their "queen," "legend," "mother" in the same sentence: *"These Charli singles so far, not doing it for me whatsoever but she's still in my mother list."*

"The Mother List." The cremains of a dead mother. Celebrity stans' tempestuous vacillations between adoration and retribution are indeed connected to mothering. One study from the mid-2000s found a correlation between celebrity stalking behavior and insecure parent-child attachment. A similar survey out of Hong Kong analyzed 401 Chinese secondary school students and identified that parental absence exacerbated participants' inclinations toward celebrity worship. A pair of studies from 2020 and 2022 confirmed that young people lacking in "positive stressors" from real-life activities and family members were poised to fixate on media surrogates. According to the latter study, early-life isolation may cause emotional deficits that can make someone more likely to focus on "trauma in the virtual world," dividing famous figures into immaculate saints and disgraced demons (in psychology literature, this is called "splitting"). "The traumas of everyday life can easily make us feel like a motherless child," said psychotherapist Mark Epstein.

It's really no wonder, then, that so many Taylor Swift acolytes slip into the "Borderline-Pathological" category of standom. With Swift's sundry albums, each of which offers not only new music, but a new "era"—a rich wellspring of aesthetics and rituals in which to steep (the small-town innocence of her self-titled debut, the vampiric vengefulness of *Reputation*, the nostalgic fantasy of *Folklore*)—she's built a whole cinematic universe of mothers. It makes as much sense that pop idols' queer stans are sometimes their most zealous, so often deprived of the parental support and acceptance they need.

In 2023, *New Yorker* music journalist Amanda Petrusich reviewed Taylor Swift's billion-dollar Eras Tour. In her analysis of the bash, she remarked that while Swifties' online possessiveness seems "both mighty and frightening," it took a totally different shape in person. Amid the rabble of rainbow sequins and ecstasy (the feeling, not the drug), Petrusich could see how protecting a sense of Swiftie solidarity could drive someone to delirium. She wrote, "Community, one of our most elemental human pleasures, has been decimated by COVID, politics, technology, capitalism . . . Swift's performance might be fixed, perfect, but what happens in the crowd is messy, wild, benevolent, and beautiful." As diverting as online gathering spaces can be, they are no stand-in for the real stuff, which is why virtual fan interactions can turn so brutal and hallucinatory. Captioning an Instagram carousel from the road, Swift posted, "This tour has become my entire personality." How could a fan know Swift wholly, then defend or chastise her accordingly, if after so many years of conflating her personas both on and offstage, Swift might not even fully know herself?

In 2003, a survey of 833 Chinese teenagers found that those who "worshipped" people they really knew, like parents and teachers who could make tangible contributions to their lives, had overall higher self-esteem and educational achievement. Glorifying pop stars and athletes predicted the opposite—lower confidence, weaker sense of self. This finding supports the "absorption addiction model" of celebrity worship, which suggests that stans pursue parasocial relationships to make up for shortages within their real lives, but in their attempts to establish personal identities through standom, they wind up losing themselves. When the modern mind is starved of nourishment, sometimes it tries to nurse in uncanny places where no milk can be found.

In both private and public spheres, worship is dehumanizing. To be deified is not so flattering; the dynamic risks annihilating a person's room for complexity and blunders, and this sets up everyone for suffering. Overanalyze a mortal's words like biblical scripture, only to find out the interpretations were false, and you can start a crusade. When stans feel betrayed by their heroes, they often revolt. And punishments are not distributed equally. With few exceptions, female idols—the "mothers"—suffer the harshest penance for the mildest crimes. And the more marginalized a female celebrity is, the less humanity we allow. I wonder, if Taylor Swift instead of Beyoncé had gone on *Good Morning America* to announce a new "vegan era," would stans have behaved as caustically? As Canadian political columnist Sabrina Maddeaux wrote in 2016, "Women, who are objects of simultaneous worship and disgust in the public eye, become both victim and villain."

Queer music journalists have noted a sinister misogyny underlying certain gay male consumers' engagement with female pop icons. Women artists have long offered fans a kind of mouthpiece for a femininity they couldn't always express. With meme culture and Twitter belligerence, this treatment has grown even more denigrating. "Once we may have merely ventriloquized women's voices as our own. Now, we speak over them," said queer entertainment critic Jared Richards.

In my own family, my attitude toward my mother was once not so different from that of a rabid celebrity worshipper. Growing up, whenever either of my parents exhibited any hint of human fallibility, I always felt twice as acrimonious toward Denise. Posed on a higher and narrower pedestal, she simply had further to fall. A few years before I graduated high school, after a nasty spat where I excoriated my mother for (god forbid) "acting so aloof all the time," she started emailing me long letters. Like a pen pal, for months, Denise shared a series of confessional memoirs from her life before I was born, stories she'd never felt comfortable divulging before. These stories, mostly about her vibrant love life, are not mine to tell, but they were crucially humanizing. They didn't extinguish my mother's halo; rather, they lit up the environment around her, so I could appreciate the context. Grasping her in more dimensions alleviated some pressure. With time, communication, and empathy, Denise and I were able to see one another more completely.

Stans treat famous women with all the veneration and vitriol of a mother, but parasocial as the relationship is, it can never truly feed them. The mob can demand catchier singles, more progressive politics, and restitution for the concert tickets their years of loyalty earned them; however, I'm skeptical that any kind of public response, inherently removed as it would be, could be satiating enough to thwart the cycle of worship and dethronement.

Naturally, we like it when our heroes are a little bit relatable. Daintily human. When a pop star forgets the opening line to her own song and has to start again. When the president sneaks a cigarette. When your mom gets a little tipsy on vacation. Like sea salt on a chocolate chip cookie, the garnish of imperfection brings out their holiness even more. But when it comes to people on pedestals, sometimes the fullness of their humanity feels like it just might kill us.

Last spring, I was comparing childhoods over lunch with a British novelist, when she brought up the concept of the "good enough mother." In 1953, English pediatrician and psychoanalyst Donald Winnicott coined this term after observing that children actually benefit when their mothers fail them in manageable ways. "Even if it were somehow possible to be the perfect mother, the end result would be a delicate, fragile child who couldn't tolerate even the slightest disappointment," summarized Dr. Carla Naumburg, a clinical social worker and author of *You Are Not a Sh*tty Parent*. "If we are good enough—which I believe most of us are—then we mostly get it right, and sometimes we get it wrong." A stan who paints their idol as a flawless mother figure seems bound for fragility. I wonder if our artistic icons just need to be *good enough*.

In some parts of the animal kingdom, species engage in filial cannibalism, where a mother eats her own young. But there's also matriphagy, or mother-eating, which is found in some insects, spiders, scorpions, and nematode worms. Crab spider mothers supply their young with unfertilized eggs to eat, but it's not enough. Over the course of several weeks, the baby spiders also eat their mother. It's a sacrifice that aids the next generation: Spiderlings that engage in mother-eating turn out with higher body weights and survival odds than those that don't. *Rolling Stone* called 2022 "The Year of the Cannibal." Hollywood produced a stunning surplus of cannibal-themed media: Hulu's *Fresh*, Showtime's *Yellowjackets*, Netflix's *Dahmer—Monster: The Jeffrey Dahmer Story*, Luca Guadagnino's *Bones and All*. Like the spiders, we were clearly starved of something: connection and protection, selfhood and guidance—the most human nutrition. We were ravenous. Some couldn't help themselves. But the celebrity matriphagy was never enough. It didn't make anyone stronger, because the stars weren't our mothers. They were made of pixels and maladaptive daydreams. The hatchlings could devour leg after leg of the mother spider, and never get full.

TWO

I SWEAR I MANIFESTED THIS
A note on proportionality bias

I was a conspiracy theorist once. Sometimes I still am. "The universe is out to get me" was practically my tagline during the restless decade of my adolescence, when it felt like the only sensible explanation for why I felt so insecure all the time had to be a cosmic plot against me. What is a conspiracy theory other than the intuition that some powerful force is out there plotting to sabotage you . . . or save you? The psychological craving for big events (and big feelings) to have equally big causes is instinctive. It's called *proportionality bias*—and while behavioral economists regard this inclination as the driving force behind extreme conspiracy theories like QAnon, it fools even the most rational minds into overestimating cause-and-effect relationships. Proportionality bias explains how "The Manifestation Doctor" got so popular on Instagram. As of the 2020s, manifestation may very well be the slyest conspiracy theory of them all.

✳ ✳ ✳

"If we could sum up *the healing* in a single short phrase, what would that be?" asks the famous pseudo-therapist known online as @TheManifestationDoctor.* Her tie-dye headscarf contrasts skin the color of raw cashews. Her voice, stage frightful and coated in a blue-collar Boston accent, doesn't match the self-actualized, just-back-from-Tibet vibe of her posts, but this perfectly imperfect everywoman schtick is part of her charm. For the past two years, the once licensed psychologist turned "holistic mental health influencer" has offered followers newly interested in therapy, but either unable or unwilling to access traditional treatment, the opportunity to learn about "Shadow Work," the "Mother Wound," and "how to regulate your nervous system without pharmaceuticals"—all in the form of bite-size explainergrams. Ensconced before a high-tech audio rig, The Manifestation Doctor is currently livestreaming a virtual launch event for her million-dollar new self-help book, *The Art of Self-Healing: Release Your Trauma and Manifest a New You*. At the time of this broadcast in 2021, her online following has ballooned to four million. She proceeds to answer her own question: "I'll give you two words that those who've been following me for a while have heard me say a million times: *holistic self-empowerment*."

---

* Several names, places, and other identifying details in this chapter, including this one, have been changed. And let me tell you, coming up with a halfway intelligible Instagram handle that wasn't already taken proved to be one of the most harrowing creative challenges of this book.

Precisely 117 of the Instagram accounts I personally follow are following @TheManifestationDoctor: old coworkers and classmates, well-known activists and authors, the singer-songwriter I listened to as I brushed my teeth this morning, my favorite neighborhood barista. I do not follow the page, not from my public account, anyway, but I have been surveilling it for about a year now from a fake profile christened after an old pet and a street I used to live on, like a porn star name. I cannot get over how big The Manifestation Doctor has gotten since the start of the pandemic, blowing up from an out-of-practice shrink with a lapsed Massachusetts license to a bona fide Dr. Phil–type star living in a mansion by the beach. It was an impressive business pivot, no doubt; I'm simply unsettled that marketing psychospirituality to millions of internet strangers became such big business at all. The Manifestation Doctor's fortune cookie advice features absolutist maxims no other therapist I cross-checked for this chapter would dare make in public: "People pleasing is unconscious manipulation"; "Overexplaining yourself is a trauma response that stems from an unresolved childhood fear of conflict"; "Disease doesn't run in families, habits do." Such sentiments seem like digestible sugar cubes of wisdom, but dispersed en masse by a mind-body hotshot, they risk aggravating anxious followers' existing concerns about their own minds. "We tend not to speak in absolutes like that," explained Dr. Aaron Weiner, an Illinois board-certified psychologist, on a phone call in mid-2021.

The scale of The Manifestation Doctor's growth was unique; her message, however, was not. At its core, in my opinion, it met all the basic criteria of a conspiracy theory. A classic story of good and evil rebranded for the modern mental health crisis, her fundamental thesis was that traditional therapy and medications are keeping you unwell, but you can self-heal your way out. You just have to learn how to make the universe bend in your favor. Sick? Poor? Not living your best life? Don't blame your mean boss or abusive ex. That's what victims do. Don't blame the blood-drinking elites, that's what *actual* conspiracy theorists do. Instead, blame your unresolved childhood trauma. And then, for $26 a month, enlist in this "self-empowerment circle," where you'll learn how to manifest the life you deserve for a fraction of the cost of traditional therapy.

This basic pitch was presented not just by The Manifestation Doctor, but by a whole class of New Age mental health figures who surged into the market throughout the early 2020s. In the US the nation's psychological state was in collective nosedive; increasing mental health discourse made folks who'd never been interested in therapy before hyperaware of their malaise. Between March 2020 and September 2022, Pew Research data found that 58 percent of adults ages eighteen to twenty-nine had experienced high levels of psychological distress. But licensed therapists across the country were either too expensive or overbooked to accept new clients. So patients started looking for solutions with less paperwork. In 2022, *The New York Times* reported that teenagers self-misdiagnosing mental disorders on TikTok had become a grave concern. American life had grown so psychologically disorienting that fringe paranoias were passing as conventional wisdom: In July 2020, Pew Research determined that 20 percent of Americans, both liberal and conservative, suspected COVID-19 was manufactured at least partially on purpose. An NPR/Ipsos poll revealed that 17 percent of respondents believed the QAnon claim that "Satan-worshiping elites who run a child sex ring are trying to control our politics and media," and another 37 percent said they "didn't know" if the myth was true or not. The term "conspirituality," a portmanteau of "conspiracy theory" and "spirituality," went from a niche academic term to a subject of popular discussion in magazine op-eds and top-charting podcasts. On January 6, 2021, the "QAnon Shaman" made headlines for invading the U.S. Capitol in a horned headdress and pagan body art. Suddenly, the once unfathomable image of young mothers in hand-dyed tunics marching shoulder to shoulder with Holocaust deniers—all united in the fight for a "paradigm shift" away from the government's totalitarian plot—became a widely recognized archetype, our new reality.

By The Manifestation Doctor's rise to fame, trust in the U.S. healthcare establishment, which was supposed to keep us safe from things like deadly plagues, had fractured so severely that plenty of citizens didn't even want conventional shrinks. They were sick to death of red tape, insurance policies, and waffling chief medical advisers in $2,000 suits. They wanted a relatable populist who spoke their language, and whom they could access for free on their phones, to tell them in certain terms that there was one big, on-purpose reason why they were feeling terrible and the world couldn't breathe, not a haphazard miscellany of tiny reasons that looked different for everyone. Consumers clung like baby marsupials to this crop of influencers whose definitions of "unresolved trauma" provided a cause for followers' distress that felt proportional to its magnitude.

The term "conspiracy theorist" does not typically trigger images of beloved therapists with book deals and celebrity fans. Until recently, I was under the impression that conspiracy theorists were either incels with rattails and UFO obsessions or Facebook-addicted Karens who think essential oils are a personality trait and vaccines make you gay. My understanding was that conspiracy theorists don't have friends or jobs, much less Ivy League degrees, millions of followers, and large publishing contracts. They spend their days on 4chan, exchanging "proof" that the moon landing was faked, 9/11 was an inside job, climate change is a hoax, the CIA killed JFK, the Royal Family killed Princess Diana, Avril Lavigne is dead, Steve Jobs is alive, and Katy Perry is actually JonBenét Ramsey all grown up. They're convinced that the earth is flat and Bill Gates is a satanist, and studies disproving their "theories"* are not compelling, because scientists are mind-controlled lizards.

These are flashy examples. No matter the political flavor, though, a conspiracy theory can be defined as a sense-making narrative that offers a satisfying explanation for some

---

* I always found the term *conspiracy* "theory" overly flattering. Special relativity is a theory. The Big Bang is a theory. That aliens helped build Stonehenge? Not a "theory."

confounding turn of events. Such incidents can be either global or personal, anything from a pandemic to financial collapse to a sudden bout of depression. In 2019, a British review of the current literature on proportionality bias gathered that "small, mundane explanations for important events" (e.g., Princess Diana died because her limo driver was drunk and speeding to avoid paparazzi) are generally not as satiating as more dramatic explanations (she was murdered by the British government). In spirit as in aesthetics, the human mind enjoys harmonious proportions: faces that meet the golden ratio, photography that follows the rule of thirds. Anyone who's ever come up with a sensational origin story for a high-stakes outcome—certainly negative ones like "Big Pharma is hiding the cure for cancer" but also positive narratives like "I manifested my success"— has a pinch of conspiracy theorist in them.

Natural selection favored a paranoid mindset. For survival, the brain evolved for an environment replete with unseen dangers and hostile intentions. To detect meaningful patterns in a topsy-turvy world became a unique human forte, but sometimes, we take it too far. Anyone is capable of drawing an oversimplified conclusion about cause and effect if it matches their preexisting worldview. The same bias that convinces QAnoners the "elites" are covertly trafficking children is also what pressures prosecutors to bring home quick, splashy guilty verdicts for high-profile criminal cases, satisfying the public's hunger for a singular supervillain to blame. I think of the infamous Amanda Knox case: In 2007, the Seattle-born twenty-year-old was studying in Perugia, Italy, when her flatmate was murdered, a crime for which Knox was swiftly and ostentatiously convicted (labeled a "Satanic," "sex-crazed" killer with "eyes of ice"), despite flagrant deficiencies in evidence. Knox was acquitted and freed in 2011, but a shocking percentage of the European public remains convinced of her guilt. Big tragedy, big blue eyes, big press treatment, big punishment. Her fate was simply proportional.

On a more private stage, proportionality bias shows up in our lives every day. An acquaintance told me she recites the same incantation every time she boards an airplane, because even though she doesn't sincerely believe in prayer, it's not worth skipping the ritual to test its relationship to her safety. After her husband's death, Joan Didion refused to give away his shoes, spiritually convinced that if the loafers remained in their proper place, he might return. I don't consider myself a superstitious person, but whenever I experience a stroke of dumb luck, my natural inclination is to pinpoint some astral rationale behind it, like the only "reason" I found $20 in my pocket or was offered a free éclair at the coffee shop this morning was because I'd let someone merge in front of me at rush hour on the way there. In virtually every context, we cannot seem to rest until we find some intentional force either to fault for our misery or credit for our success. The greater the effect, the greater we desire the cause to be.

Paranoia is a profitable disposition. While the belief that our government is running villainous underground mind control labs might be a smidge far-fetched for most, you can build a whole brand on the suggestion that your own diseased brain is to blame for your poor health and dwindling bank account. During the mental health crisis of the early 2020s, hundreds of "holistic" wellness brands seized the public's proportionality bias by the gonads. In COVID lockdown, a close friend of mine joined To Be Magnetic, a self-help program led by Lacy Phillips, a struggling actress turned "Neural Manifestation Adviser." Phillips, who does not have any sort of therapy accreditation but lots of wide-brim hats, claims to specialize in "unblocking" your "subconscious self-sabotage" through "deep imaginings," where followers learn to "reprogram old memories" in order to "align with what they truly desire." In 2022, I learned of Peoplehood, a "therapeutic but not therapy" business from the founders of SoulCycle that organizes group oversharing events, like a slumber party-meets-AA meeting. At Peoplehood, hour-long spill sessions labeled "gathers" invite strangers to divulge their darkest fears and loftiest goals to each other, supervised not by licensed counselors but by performers recruited as "guides" and described by *The New York Times* as "charisma bombs." The same year Peoplehood launched, so did Munko, an exclusive, NFT-powered artist collective on Discord (what a time to be alive). Founded and helmed by controversial artist David Choe, Munko beckoned a devoted, mostly male audience to "surrender" their most shameful failures and heal through Choe's pithy tips for overcoming addiction and self-loathing. And in yet another pocket of the New Age sphere, inspirational life coaches like Jay Shetty and Gabrielle Bernstein were turning their cult followings into multimedia empires. Powered by a BFA in theater and an endorsement from Oprah, Bernstein penned the *New York Times* bestseller *The Universe Has Your Back* and produced podcasts on "how to talk to angels" and become "a Major Manifestor." Shetty, whom I can only think to describe as a "male girlboss," authored the self-help blockbuster *Think Like a Monk* (though he is not himself a monk), stating on JayShetty.Me that his purpose is "to make wisdom go viral."

This is just a tiny sampling of the mental health influencers who found a modern audience—never mind all the aspirants. As I was writing this chapter, feeling fidgety and unsure if my argument even made sense, I checked my Instagram notifications to find a new comment from an account called @priestess_naomi_. The profile picture displayed a white woman with snaking blond extensions and a rhinestone bindi. Her bio read, "Healer, Pure Bioenergy Therapist, Soulmate and twin flame expert, spiritual coach, mother of one, daughter of light." The priestess's comment: "I see glory and blessings in you and you are destined for greatness directly from birth. I have an important message but I will need your honest permission to proceed because your ancestors have been trying to reach you by revealing some signs to you, maybe through your dreams, or the repeated numbers that you normally see (222,4:44,1111,15:15) . . . I also see your throat and sacral energy blocked. So kindly reply once you get this message with a picture of your right hand palm, my dear, if you want to know the message I have for you. Namaste." Sometimes, after tossing around an idea to death, I'll start to think I've lost my mind and have nothing to say. You could call this comment from Priestess Naomi "a sign from the universe" to keep writing. All I had to do was check Instagram to find it.

While men's tastes in conspiracy theories often point them in the direction of UFOs and satanic cabals, educated women are more likely than anyone to embrace New Age concepts, like moon bathing, crystal healing, and manifestation techniques, including the law of attraction*. Combining mysticism with polysyllabic DSM buzzwords like "dysregulated," "neural pathways," "epigenetics," and "vasovagal response," these teachings feel like a delicious cross between a tarot reading and a medical diagnosis. At first blush, promises of self-healing seem empowering: While classic conspiracy theories place followers' loci of control entirely outside themselves, blaming external forces (the government, the "elites") for whatever happens, manifestation redirects loci of control back to the individual. I find this flip of the script even more insidious. Most conspiracy theories argue that a mysterious outside evil is trying to control you. By contrast, *conspiracy therapy* says that the evil force is your own mind.

"Self-healing" is a New Age abstraction that commodifies the Tibetan Buddhist teaching that we all create our

---

* Emerging in the late nineteenth century from the New Thought movement, this pseudo-scientific perspective argues that positive or negative thoughts bring on either positive or negative experiences. Many hit self-help books riff on this "law," including 1952's *The Power of Positive Thinking* by Norman Vincent Peale (Donald Trump's childhood pastor) and the 2006 mega-bestseller *The Secret* by Australian TV producer turned world-famous spiritual diva, Rhonda Byrne.

own destinies. The original tenet says that we may not be able to control other people or events, but with our own reactions, we can abate suffering. One problem with the neatly-packaged-for-Instagram version of this principle is that it can lead to an obsessive focus on personal responsibility. A key message of conspiracy therapy centers on the universal dangers of "trauma," framed, simplistically, as unhealed wounds from childhood. Certain influencers have overgeneralized the link between unresolved trauma and disease (a teaching which starts to feel especially hairy when you consider, say, childhood cancers). This flattened attitude toward suffering discounts systemic factors, like medical racism or generational poverty, as well as random misfortune, which may or may not be traumatic. Equally, it over-credits personal efforts for auspicious outcomes.

The tendency to explain away complex issues with metaphysical doctrine is sometimes labeled "spiritual bypassing." Covertly, this outlook discourages people from seeking external care, like medication or even support from loved ones, since its underlying tenet says misery is yours alone to attract or repel. Its popularity has made psychologists' clinical work more challenging. Dr. Suraji Wagage, a licensed clinical psychologist based in Los Angeles, told me in 2023 that treating disorders like OCD, PTSD, and depression "is (and has been) harder" when clients show up to one-on-one therapy with "only inaccurate, sometimes insulting, stereotypes about what they mean." That's if a client makes their way off social media at all. Rather than providing a helpful starter pack of resources for followers to carry into the real world, some mental health accounts establish a guru-style power dynamic. "On the surface, it can *seem* like [they're] empowering the reader with information, but it risks building a kind of psychological dependence on the content creator . . . If I teach you how to think for yourself, you don't need me anymore, and I'm out of business," offered Dr. Dena DiNardo, a Pennsylvania-based licensed psychologist and family therapist. But these possibilities are not obvious at first. Unless you're a trained practitioner, you might scroll through an engaging explainer carousel about attachment theory without picking up the conspiratorial attitude between the lines.

A new follower of The Manifestation Doctor might not immediately find that their new favorite wellness expert was connected to a clique of much more violent conspiracy theorists. A few clicks away from her heavily monitored comments section would reveal a disquieting subplot: In establishing her brand and website, The Manifestation Doctor took cues from Kelly Brogan, known as the "Holistic Psychiatrist." The Center for Countering Digital Hate, a British nonprofit, named Brogan one of the "Disinformation Dozen," a group of twelve people responsible for spreading 65 percent of all vaccine-related misinformation online. Brogan has falsely claimed that coffee enemas treat depression and infectious disease is caused by mental illness rather than pathogens (controversially, she also served as a "functional medicine expert" and "trusted contributor" to Gwyneth Paltrow's Goop). Throughout the pandemic, The Manifestation Doctor openly supported content from alt-right extremists, like Sean Whalen, a men's rights influencer and owner of the clothing brand Lions Not Sheep, known for its "Give Violence a Chance" message tees (which attracted a $211,000 FTC fine for containing bogus "Made in the USA" tags). Often pictured holding machine guns, or posting images of Jesus holding machine guns, Whalen endorsed "real masculinity" as a prevention against COVID, declaring that medical masks were for "little bitch asses." In 2021, The Manifestation Doctor's media manager spent many weeks promoting a crowdfunding campaign for a Michigan gym owner and Holocaust denier to pay for state fines he incurred after establishing a "no masks allowed" rule at his gym and promising free memberships to anyone who renounced vaccination.

Not every member of a New Age therapy group will end up in "no masks allowed" territory. However, their doctrine remains dangerous because of how conspiracy theories function. When an influential figure cracks your faith in one foundational idea—be it as broad as "the media" or as specific as "antidepressants"—suspicion seeps in like root rot. Radical conspiracism might start with "the art of self-healing," but from there, the "vaccine awareness movement" is not too far a leap, and before you know it, well, how *do* we know the moon landing wasn't faked?

These risks are not theoretical. I spoke to a few of The Manifestation Doctor's early admirers, for whom the account ended up being a direct QAnon gateway. Like Heather, a new mother, who found The Manifestation Doctor in 2019. At the time, the account only had around fifty thousand followers. Heather was struggling with postpartum depression and didn't have much support. The child of absentee addicts, she was drawn to The Manifestation Doctor's succinct discussions of codependency, attachment theory, and the idea that one could DIY their own brain chemistry like an IKEA dresser. "I was trying to understand my dysfunctional upbringing while navigating parenthood myself," Heather said. "The account made me feel empowered, like there was a reason I was suffering."

A few weeks after following The Manifestation Doctor, Heather mentioned the account to her dad as something he might enjoy. Having spent a tumultuous childhood in the LDS church and an adulthood in and out of rehab, Heather's father was finally sober for the longest stretch of his life. He had begun therapy and antidepressants for the first time. "I started to see the light in his eyes," Heather recalled. Committed to his new healing journey, he created an Instagram account just so he could follow The Manifestation Doctor. He'd never used social media before. "I feel so guilty about that now," says Heather. Within six months, Heather's dad had entered QAnon waters. If far-right conspiracy theories were the open ocean, social media algorithms were the rip tide, and The Manifestation Doctor's posts were tempting wavelets lapping at the shoreline. Things took a turn when Heather's dad joined the "Self-Empowerment Circle," her online subscription community. For $26 a month, devout manifesters could ostensibly learn what her most transformative version of "the healing" looked like. Her father enlisted and stopped taking his medication shortly thereafter. "In The Manifestation Doctor's world, [antidepressants] dull your senses," Heather recalled. Her dad announced that he didn't need therapy anymore because he was doing "the healing" instead. "Whatever 'the healing' is," said Heather. "He never gave a definitive answer."

One weekend in mid-2020, Heather's dad accompanied her and her kids on a camping trip. While sitting around the fire, he asked if she'd heard about the "elites who drink blood to stay young." Heather recounted, "He stopped and looked at me like I was the crazy one who wasn't 'awakened' to all this." Shortly after that trip, her father's life was fully consumed by right-wing conspiracy theories. The last time Heather saw him was Thanksgiving 2020. "He's still really disconnected from reality," she said. "That light in his eyes is just gone."

In the two decades between 9/11 and COVID-19, paranoia tendriled through America's morale like a fungus. In 2018, MIT found that true stories take six times longer to reach 1,500 people on Twitter than false ones. That's because "false news is more novel, and people are more likely to share novel information. People who share novel information are seen as being in the know," said Sinan Aral, the study's coauthor. Conspiracy therapists are not motivated to share nuanced facts, but rather content that will paint them as supremely wise. One-sided sentiments like "Overexplaining yourself is a trauma response that stems from an unresolved childhood fear of conflict" are far better for engagement than

"People justify their actions in different ways for different reasons," or "All traumatic events are stressful, but not all stressful events are traumatic." Furthermore, information transmission research suggests that folks with higher anxiety are quicker to engage with, and slower to disengage from, negative information; so, "as a trait and state," anxiety itself perpetuates paranoid thinking.

Certainly, social media therapists with pure intentions and careful executions exist. They are forthright about what posts contain facts versus anecdotes, and their presence helps destigmatize mental healthcare. However, some experts still feel squirmy about the mix of brain health and brand building. "Therapists are taking their branding into their own hands, but the problem is the lack of checks and balances," said Dr. DiNardo. The blend of medicine and self-marketing is indeed an awkward modern revelation. It defies the "no advertising rule" from the American Medical Association's original Code of Ethics, which was written in 1847 and remained unchanged for over a century. The Food and Drug Administration has the authority to castigate famous medical doctors when they espouse misinformation, as they did in 2011 when TV superstar Dr. Oz claimed there were dangerous levels of arsenic in apple juice, sending mothers around the country into needless panic. But unlike celebrity physicians, there's actually no clear way to crack down on cult-followed psychologists.

Malpractice in behavioral health, Dr. Aaron Weiner told me, is "a very hazy concept." With psychotherapy, there aren't the same treatment algorithms used for diagnosing and treating, say, an infection or back pain. "If someone has a license to practice therapy in the state, they can basically do that however they want," Weiner said. Even if they tout harmful advice and an ethics complaint is filed, unless there was some clear legal breach like sexual assault, it's tough to strip someone of their license. The success of brands like Peoplehood, To Be Magnetic, and The Manifestation Doctor demonstrates that accreditation doesn't always matter anyway. And good luck holding an influencer accountable for practicing bad "therapy." As far as social media companies are concerned, the more viral wellness quacks, the better. "It's actually a bit of an issue," Weiner continued. "And it bridges into this question of, do we need more gatekeepers in behavioral health?"

Alternative mental health influencers are alluring, because most of them mean well enough, and they're right about a lot of things. Beliefs about yourself *do* influence outcomes. Spirituality *is* shown to increase resilience. You *can* alter your reactions to certain stressors. Big Pharma *has* made grave mistakes. Some medications *have* been irresponsibly prescribed. Marginalized populations have innumerable reasons to mistrust the mental health establishment. And we need translators who can bring psychology concepts down from the high shelf of academia to the public. "The easiest lies to believe are the ones closest to the truth," said Weiner, who likened tumbling down a conspiratorial rabbit hole to falling into drug addiction. "Few people start by injecting heroin, but if you use recreational drugs, eventually you might get there," he said. "That may be part of what we're looking at with spiritual pseudopsychology. In small imperceptible increments, you work your way toward something you would've never believed if it had been proposed to you in the first place."

In 2018, I enrolled in therapy for the first time. I'd just gotten out of a relationship in which I'd developed a host of bad communication habits—skittishness around confrontation, defensiveness. I wanted to learn how to minimize toting that baggage into my future partnerships. After trying on a few therapists, I eventually found the right one for my disposition, but I'll never forget the very first practitioner I met because, and pardon my candor, she immediately struck me as a woo-woo schmuck. Based in Venice, California, the counselor's office was festooned with beads and geodes, and at one point, she mentioned goat yoga as a treatment for PTSD. This therapist was recommended to me by name, so clearly she clicked with someone, but it only took one $175 session for me to conclude the gal was not for me. That's the thing with one-on-one therapy—you know exactly where your information is coming from, because you can see the person sitting in front of you with your own two eyes. They're not a "brand." They're a licensed professional, who (hopefully) pays close attention to your individual needs and responds accordingly to the best of their ability. And odds are, you've paid more than you care to for the honor, so if their style rubs you the wrong way, your tolerance for that isn't going to be very high. But at the internet's all-you-can-eat buffet, where cherry-picking what resonates is as easy as the upward flick of a thumb, you could spiral into conspiratorial delusion and not even notice. Proportionality bias does the work for you. And while adding more prescriptions won't single-handedly fix every modern mental struggle, neither will seeking alternatives in the artificial spaces that inflamed them to begin with. Paying a wealthy stranger $26 a month for their dubious online manifestation course is just a version of Stockholm syndrome.

Far from Instagram therapy, in certain collectivist indigenous cultures, perceiving intentionality in one's environment fosters not paranoia about the universe, but rather harmony with it. This perspective, called "animism," proposes that a tree is not a soulless piece of furniture; it's more like a roommate, or even a parent. Everything in the world has an innate "personhood," which is connected to all others, and failing to respect that risks crashing nature's cosmic economy. Laura Giles, a Virginia-based licensed clinical social worker, suggests that ascribing intentionality to external events and objects—to think that the flowers do not "want" to be picked, the car is "telling you" it needs maintenance—is a natural, healthy way to interpret the world. But it can be corrupted. Combine our organic animism with capitalism and tech-powered misinformation spread, and you get conspirituality.

"I'm going to get in trouble for saying this, but I think the law of attraction is largely based on fantasy, and I don't think we should encourage that," said Giles, who comes from an animist background. Giles's mother emigrated to the American South from an Asian indigenous community and raised her daughter to perceive an animating spirit everywhere. "Thoughts do create reality, but we live in a physical world and have to obey the laws of nature. You can't do something spiritual and expect it to manifest in the real world like that," she said.

To Be Magnetic's founder Lacy Phillips claims her "proprietary" manifestation technique is "backed by neuroscience, psychology, EMDR, epigenetics, and energetics with a little spirituality sprinkled on top." She says the method is "based on raising your self-worth and stepping into your unique authenticity by reprogramming the subconscious limiting beliefs that you picked up during childhood and throughout your life." The Manifestation Doctor defines her titular practice as "the simple process of purposefully calling whatever it is you want into your life. . . . All you need is a bit of practice to alter your mindset into actively creating rather than passively receiving what happens to you."

In the spirit of trouble, I might as well admit that I think "manifestation" is often little more than a combination of proportionality bias, confirmation bias, and *frequency bias*. Also known as the "Baader-Meinhof phenomenon," frequency bias is an attention filter that explains the common experience of taking note of something once and then miraculously seeing it again and again. You hear a song for the first time, and suddenly it's everywhere. Your favorite musician died on April 21—now the numbers 4 and 21 appear wherever you turn, a sign from the great beyond. You learn what frequency bias is, and boom, everyone is talking about it.* Unless a "holistic" mental health figure is actively guarding against this powerful trio of biases, then I'm quite willing to believe they genuinely stand by their own doctrine. If we're primed to think that big effects have big causes, and to hallucinate patterns everywhere we look, then of course we'll believe the reason why failure no longer follows us is because we learned to control the fate of the universe.

"The universe has your back" sounds like a positive affirmation. But to me, it's still a conspiracy theory, because it plays into the narrative that the universe cares—that it could be out to get you if it wanted to. Nature does not "care" like that. If it has intentions, they're not of the human kind.

I think of the Northern Lights, those kaleidoscopic neon ribbons that glint across the Arctic sky at certain times of year. The lights are so magnificent, they seem to be putting on a show for us. But they aren't theater—they're a product of violence and defense. When mighty solar windstorms catapult from the sun toward earth like an electric slingshot, our planet's upper atmosphere acts as an invisible force field, protecting us down on the surface. When those winds slam into earth's calm shield, the aurora forms, and

---

* How's this for a healthcare conspiracy: Frequency bias can cause medical doctors to over-diagnose a condition just because they've recently read up on it. In 2019, a med student named Kush Purohit sent a letter of concern about frequency bias to the editor of *Academic Radiology*, reporting that after he learned of a condition called "bovine aortic arch," he happened to discover three more cases of it within the next twenty-four hours.

the more dangerous the storm, the more stunning the light show. It's a war up there, but also gorgeous in its brutality. Nature just does what it does, and sometimes it's ruinous, but it doesn't mean for it to be. It doesn't "mean" anything at all. Meaning is *our* job.

By all means, let's have our spiritual lens, but if it's too opaque, we won't be able to see what others see. In his book *The Myth of Normal*, trauma specialist Dr. Gabor Maté wrote, "We are steeped in the normalized myth that we are, each of us, mere individuals striving to attain private goals. The more we define ourselves that way, the more estranged we become from vital aspects of who we are and what we need to be healthy."

What if the universe isn't for or against us? What if it's not that serious? What if the bakery just made too many éclairs, and I only got a free one so it wouldn't go to waste? The chocolate ganache tastes like magic either way.

THREE

A Toxic Relationship Is Just a Cult of One
A note on the sunk cost fallacy

This is a story about the most irrational thing I've ever done. It's also an attempt to make sense of it, even forgive it.

Much has been written in the areas of psychology and self-help seeking to explain the truly unhinged behavioral patterns humans exhibit in defense of their romantic relationships, including and especially the horrible ones. Partnerships can be pure misery, and still, many of us are practically allergic to ending them. By way of explanation, there's talk of trauma and cycles of abuse. There's talk of destroyed self-esteem and fear of retaliation. Then, among behavioral economists, there's talk of the *sunk cost fallacy*: the deeply ingrained conviction that spending resources you can't get back—money and time but also emotional resources, like secrets and hope—justifies spending even more. It is this explanation that jigsaw-clicked into place what I was never able to understand about my choice to stay in a relationship that caused me great suffering for seven of my formative years.

Reading the literature doesn't change what happened, but the facts are encouragingly consistent enough that they might change what happens next. "In times of trouble, I had been trained since childhood, read, learn, work it up. . . . Information was control," Didion said. Or at least the illusion of control. When you fix your eyes carefully on one corner of a peripheral drift illusion, the psychedelic rippling stills. Only then can you begin to see what your brain didn't want to at first. Only then can you move on.

In my defense, I was so young when the love-bombing started that my potential for rationality was physiologically limited. My cheeks were still round as snow globes then, my freckles sharp as cactus needles, like they were in 4K resolution, technology that hadn't been invented yet, because it was only 2010, and I was in high school.

I got to know the man two months after my eighteenth birthday and two months before graduation. "The man," meaning my long-term ex, the older one whose name I avoid mentioning if I can help it. I've tried coming up with code names for him, partially for his anonymity but also because saying the real one still makes me queasy. My nerves remember the assortment of vowels and consonants, the stress they carried. A pseudonym tricks the body. A few years ago, I settled on the alias "Mr. Backpack," partially because, like everyone else in LA, he liked hiking, but also because the label feels neutral and nonthreatening, like a side character in a children's TV show. Symbolically it also tracks, because our relationship still weighs on my shoulders, and I look forward to the day I can finally take a load off, untie my boots, and have a chortle about the time I almost tripped and fell off an emotional cliff.

Things kicked off with Mr. Backpack my senior year, right when my teenage hope for the future was at its peak ripeness, prickly and awkward on the outside but soft and bursting with sweetness within, like a jackfruit. Still living with my parents but so close to leaving for college in New York City, the big electric island where I'd always planned to spend my adulthood, I was starved for my life to start already. I wanted something riotously exciting to bump me from the standby list onto the next flight.

The charismatic older man seemed like a pilot, offering me a first-class seat. Mr. Backpack was twenty-nine with an acerbic wit and steely eyes. Naturally, I developed a crush. He had pale skin that bore more tattoos and scars than the baby-faced boys my age, and those eyes, which crinkled when he told me I had something special to say to the world, and he'd be the one to help me figure it out.

Our flirtation began over text, while I was gearing up for finals and he was working a glamorous job in California, where he lived. At the time, though, I didn't realize we were "flirting." I'd actually encountered Mr. Backpack once before, a year earlier when I was a junior, as he was visiting my hometown. My hair was longer then, and I was still a virgin, so it felt like he'd met someone else. I remember the way he swirled his whiskey rocks. I remember his fish tales. I remember how intimidated I felt, and itchy to impress him. Half a year later, I was at a spring break slumber party when, high on nothing but 3 a.m. loopiness and too much Diet Cherry Coke, a friend helped me sleuth Mr. Backpack's number. I prank-texted him some cutesy joke about it being happy hour somewhere. When he responded, I assumed the suave Californian just found me amusing, quaint, and was kind enough to humor me with a few rounds of banter.

Even after the text messages developed into long late-night phone calls, I never considered it could be anything other than an unlikely friendship. After all, why would a man with a job and a life three thousand miles away want anything more from someone whose greatest life accomplishment had to do with an AP exam?

A few weeks in, Mr. Backpack announced on the phone that he was "interested in me romantically." My guts plummeted. "Get in line," I joked, playing some version of "cool." In reality, I was in my childhood basement, where I always took these clandestine calls, eyeing a sun-bleached eight-by-ten portrait of my grandparents, fully exiting my body. I'd never had a boyfriend before. "What are we doing here, Amanda?" he prompted. To save face, I pretended I had been in on our dalliance all along. Who was I to turn him down?

The day after my senior prom, he flew to the East Coast to sneak me off to a hotel room for the weekend, where we had sex for only the third time in my life. Drunk on half a glass of champagne, I tried to appear experienced, unruffled, though I can't imagine I pulled it off. There was no hiding it—I was a hatchling. But I'm sure that was half the appeal. I just thought it was cool that he could legally buy alcohol and book a hotel room all by himself.

The first time Mr. Backpack told me he loved me, I was out of my depth. I didn't know what romantic love was supposed to feel like, but I was worried this might be the only chance I'd ever get to experience it. So I told him I loved him back. Shortly after that, we came to an understanding that if we had any chance of working out, I'd need to move from New York to Los Angeles as soon as I finished college. So, even though I'd only just begun my freshman year, I quietly blew out the candle of my dream to become a literary writer in Manhattan and lit a new one for our future together in California, as he hated New York. I would accommodate. We couldn't break up now. There was so much left to do. We didn't have a "song." I'd never had an orgasm. My friends didn't really "get" us. Surely those experiences were to come. Weren't they?

For the next three years, instead of going out with college friends on weekends and recharging at home on semester breaks, I flew to Los Angeles to be with Mr. Backpack. Despite my mentors' advice against it, I graduated early so I could join him out there sooner.

A TOXIC RELATIONSHIP IS JUST A CULT OF ONE

Looking back, it's obvious how cultlike our dynamic was—the over-the-top attention and false promises, the harsh punishments whenever I questioned his opinions or decisions, the withdrawal from my former life. Though I wouldn't recognize all that until later. At the time, I was too starry-eyed to notice the red flags, like the way he spoke about his ex-girlfriends as if they were all malicious traitors (*I can't become just another ex*, I told myself); or when he warned me on our first trip together in 2010, a dwindling bottle of Jack Daniel's in hand, that he was a "very moody person" and I should prepare for the next downswing; or the rare visit he paid me in New York my sophomore year, when he stayed in my dorm room to save money and got so furious about having to sign in and out at the security desk whenever he went out for a smoke that he punched the elevator wall next to me until his fist bled. Our relationship was so abnormal, under such scrutiny all the time, that I never spoke an ugly word about it, not even to my closest friends. This was partially out of loyalty to Mr. Backpack, but also because I was convinced that once I put my misadventures on the record, the story would change from one of an old soul's extraordinary love to a dumb kid's choice to tolerate abuse. I didn't want that to be my story.

I don't think Mr. Backpack set out to harm anyone. I don't think he seriously considered our power dynamic at all. But after my move to Los Angeles, as I got older and more self-assured, the power scales shifted, and he got meaner. ("Go fuck yourself" and "Do you hear how stupid you sound?"

were phrases to which I became so accustomed they turned to white noise.) I told myself that pain came with the territory of a relationship like this, that I was lucky a wise older man had chosen me at all. And the longer I stayed, the more challenging things got, the more faith I placed in that notion. It felt compulsory. I was twenty-five before I finally defected.

Four years later: At twenty-nine, the very age that Mr. Backpack was when we started things, I finally decided to conduct a post-breakup autopsy. *Information was control.* I got in touch with a well-known clinical psychologist named Dr. Ramani Durvasula, author of several books, including *Should I Stay or Should I Go: Surviving a Relationship with a Narcissist*. Durvasula explained that choosing to charge past the wind farm of red flags and suffer for years in a bad relationship can be connected to an investment model. "People might think, 'I've put in all this time, I don't want to look back in twenty years and think it was all for nothing,'" she told me. Textbook sunk cost fallacy.

When we find ourselves in the middle of a losing situation—from a toxic relationship or exploitative spiritual group to something as low-stakes as a boring movie—we tend to persevere, telling ourselves that the win we expected is coming any moment now. That way, we don't have to admit to ourselves that we made a bad bet and lost. Sunk cost fallacy emerges when you feel compelled to finish all nineteen seasons of *Grey's Anatomy* even though you lost interest long ago, because you're two hundred episodes in and already paid the cable bill. Or when you're sorely losing at poker and decide to say, "Fuck it," and go all in, because you've put so much on the table already and couldn't live with yourself if you folded. The bias is tied to loss aversion, humans' spiritual allergy to facing defeat.

For seven years, I waited for my relationship with Mr. Backpack to improve, all the while telling myself that if I just committed harder, we'd eventually find our bliss. I refused to accept that things would never go back to how they were at the start or to how they were promised to be. After I got out, I beat myself up for self-deluding all those years. What kind of self-respecting person drops to their knees and begs someone who hasn't made them feel loved in almost a decade not to walk away?

In 2019, a Brown University philosophy professor named Ryan Doody theorized that while the sunk cost fallacy may be technically irrational in the context of hypothetical models and optimized outcomes, this doesn't quite hold true in a human context. In a paper titled "The Sunk Cost 'Fallacy' Is Not a Fallacy," Doody posed that it's actually reasonable enough to want to continue a project based on the time and energy you've already spent on it, given the universal motivation to create a positive impression of one's decision-making track record.

We know well by now that humans fare better in groups than they do on their own. In order to build a desirable circle of contacts (friends, colleagues, followers), we try to cast ourselves in a socially attractive light. Performing a sequence of actions that caused you suffering, like spending many years in a secretly abusive relationship (Doody calls this "diachronic misfortune"), when a different set of choices would have made you happier, is embarrassing. It's not so deluded to figure that admitting to that kind of decision may sabotage your social worth. To fess up to such a miscalculation might lead others to think you're either a loose cannon who has no idea what they want, or an incompetent hack who lost a bet—and not just any bet, a bet about yourself. It's extra humiliating to bungle a wager concerning your own emotions (rather than something external, like a poker hand), because it suggests that you aren't even predictable to you, and that won't exactly inspire confidence in others. Honoring sunk costs might make you seem more consistent, like you know yourself well and can make shrewd predictions about your happiness, which might frame you as the kind of player others will want on their team in the game of life.

The human mind is wired for judgment. A 2014 study from the *Journal of Neuroscience* found that our amygdalas make snap conclusions about whether someone appears trustworthy or not before we know who they are or even fully process what they look like. But we don't need empirical studies to know how judgy people are—we can feel it. I was barely in preschool when I first gathered that I should play up my successes and camouflage my mistakes in order to make a positive impression on others. Thanks to dating apps and social media, which make everyone's image miserably visible—subject to the harsh scrutiny of potentially

A TOXIC RELATIONSHIP IS JUST A CULT OF ONE

limitless eyeballs—we've arguably entered the judgiest era of all time. In such a critical and competitive climate, where our social value is both fragile and fleeting, people might feel extra pressure to heed their sunk costs in order to avoid admitting they screwed up. These heightened stakes are no doubt related to the fact that whenever my relationship with Mr. Backpack was at its worst, I'd post the happiest-looking photos of us online.

To appear socially valuable, we're all incentivized to seem as though we know what we want and always have, that we're adept at evaluating risks in life and at making good calls along the way. To establish such a reputation, we are each tasked with a creative challenge—to weave the many choices we've made over the years into a cohesive and flattering story about who we are. We do this almost automatically. We can't help ourselves. Come to think of it, I do it throughout this whole book.

We want others to believe a fairy-tale version of us, and we want to believe it ourselves, too. Sometimes, says Doody, sticking by your sunk costs winds up being the most "sensible" way to pen the most exonerating tale of your life, because it helps you bury any disordered plot points or character traits that could color you as the villain (or village idiot) rather than the hero. This drive to have the best kind of parable written about you, to be a character others will want in their story, is what Doody deems "universally had and deeply rooted." I'd speculate that this yearning feels even stronger for writers, or dreamers in general, who are forever narrativizing themselves. If staying in a diachronically misfortunate relationship will ultimately be good for the story, evidently we often figure, *Fine, so be it.*

It is possible that by remaining in my relationship with Mr. Backpack for so many years, I may have crafted the impression that I had my shit together, and that may have led to some social or even professional advancement in a way I'll never know. This doesn't mean I would make the same choices if I could time travel backwards, or that I "have no regrets" and that everything happened "for a reason." Regret is a natural reaction to past stumbles, and acknowledging it can help someone move forward. I know it did for me.

A bottomless well of societal factors traps people in toxic partnerships: the American government's unquestionably pro-marriage policies, our culture's remaining spinster stereotypes, and our rigid alpha male standards (which encourage men, who experience just as much emotional abuse in relationships as women, to keep their sensitivities in a vault). Romantic movies perpetuate zealous "ride or die" attitudes. Many world religions and even governments condemn divorce; as of 2022, leaving your spouse is still illegal in the Philippines. Protestant capitalism conditions Americans to regard breakups as shameful "failures," even though spending years with someone who treats your heart like a toilet plunger seems far more tragic to me. It's no wonder we stick by people who hurt us.

I have plenty of "regrets." But it comforts me to know that my choices didn't make me an indefensible numbskull.

A TOXIC RELATIONSHIP IS JUST A CULT OF ONE

They made me a social creature, full of hope, who wanted a beautiful story to be told about her. Fundamentally, that's still who I am.

In 2021, a pair of University of Virginia psychology researchers presented ninety-one participants with a pattern and asked them to make it symmetrical by either adding or removing colored blocks. They were intrigued to find that only 20 percent of participants opted to solve the problem by taking blocks away—a subtractive approach. This bias toward additive solutions is widespread, and it's connected to the loss aversion that trapped me in my relationship with Mr. Backpack. When presented with a problem, most people naturally think the cause must be that something is *missing*, rather than that something is gratuitous or out of place. Additive solution bias explains why, during a recent attempt to improve my sleep routine, I decided to spend $100 on lavender pillow spray, a tub of adaptogen powder, and a sunrise alarm clock instead of just cutting the afternoon espresso and keeping my phone out of the bedroom. I tried to add half a dozen colored blocks to solve my problem, when the answer was simply removing the two in my way.

Say you're going on a hike someone warned you was difficult. Additive solution bias is the impulse telling you to take a big water bottle, some hiking poles, and heavy-duty boots in order to get up the mountain. Once, I had to give up in the middle of a hike with Mr. Backpack and felt ashamed for months that I was too weak to summit. But when we returned later that summer, I ascended to the peak with ease.

Why? Because I left my backpack in the car. It was weighing me down. I thought the key to victory was an armory of fancy outdoor gear, but really all I needed was my own two feet.

In my relationship with Mr. Backpack, I told myself that what would heal us was a bigger apartment or a splashy vacation to shake things up. But sometimes what you actually need to be happy is to take something *away*. This inclination is especially hard to resist as consumerists, who are conditioned to believe that in order to fix something, you've got to add a gadget, an app, a supplement, a paragraph, a person, instead of stepping back, taking stock of everything in front of you, and considering that the problem might actually be solved by scaling down. Remove the colored block. Leave the cumbersome REI trappings behind. Break up.

When I think about my relationship with Mr. Backpack now, it feels like it happened to someone else long ago and far away, but my body remembers it like it happened this morning at the breakfast table. Sometimes I'll find myself plugging away on my laptop at a coffee shop, distracted, living in the future, when a passerby's voice tickles a familiar cochlear hair, or an old photo resurfaces in my iPhone Memories, sending me into a state of whiplash. Then I'll take a gulping breath and redirect my focus to how unbelievably grateful I am to be in my thirties rather than eighteen, having constructed a life that's sometimes just as painful as before, but that feels, more and more each day, like my own.

A TOXIC RELATIONSHIP IS JUST A CULT OF ONE

In the end, I made an authorly career work for me in California. Within a handful of years after Mr. Backpack and I split up, I'd published a couple of books, including the one about cults: why people join them, and why they stay.

My whole life, I'd always been fascinated by power-abusive religious leaders and the followers they attract. Growing up, I was convinced I had nothing in common with *those* people. I believed the stereotype that individuals who wind up in groups like the Manson Family and the Moonies are desperate, disturbed, or intellectually deficient. I fancied myself immune to the pernicious charms of charismatic gurus. But then I began my reporting, and I discovered that these judgments of cult followers are not only shallow assumptions, they also obscure the truth that cultlike influence shows up in places we might not think to look—our own relationships, for example—and none of us is above it.

The questions onlookers most frequently ask cult survivors sound just like the ones people asked me about Mr. Backpack: "Why did you ever get involved with him? Didn't you see the signs?" and then, "Why didn't you just leave?" I was aiming for True Love. But my youthful, romcom-conditioned optimism made me vulnerable, unable to clock the differences between romance and control, passion and chaos. All I knew was that Mr. Backpack had a sage look in his eyes and lots of promises, and I felt brave for chasing a love others might not. The audiobook of my life played on an internal loop, and it told me I was an adventurer who could thrive under extreme conditions. By no coincidence, it is so often utopian-minded folks who perceive their lives as hero's journeys, rather than "desperate" or downtrodden individuals, who wind up in socio-spiritual cults.

The term "love-bombing" has since the 1970s described cult leaders' strategic use of over-the-top affection to lure recruits into the fold. It's the same sort of campaign that, in predatory relationships, might be labeled "grooming." With cults, you hear about "mind control," and "spiritual bypassing," which effectively mean the same thing as "emotional abuse." When a cult leader requires members to fork over huge sums of money to the group, it's labeled "financial exploitation"; when a partner consumes or takes control over a partner's finances without consent, that's "domestic theft." Blackmail can work its way into toxic relationships—threats of leaking incriminating photos or messages to discourage you from leaving—and the same goes for cults. We call cult leaders "charismatic gurus," while we call abusive lovers "charming narcissists."

In cults, a process of "dehumanization" involves a leader assigning new names and uniforms to slowly strip followers of their identities. A leader might then ignore veteran members in order to focus on new recruits, which motivates existing loyalists to fight for their attention. Durvasula told me that in unhealthy partnerships, similar steps are known as the "devaluation" and "discard" phases, which might look like an abuser convincing their partner to move across the

A TOXIC RELATIONSHIP IS JUST A CULT OF ONE

country for them, dress differently, and change jobs, only then to neglect or cheat on them. Cult leaders commonly prohibit members to fraternize with outsiders or consume media that speaks ill of the group. Romantic abusers might encourage their partners to cut off friends or family members who don't "support" their love.

A toxic relationship is just a cult of one. While the framing is different, the behaviors are more or less equivalent. And as for the people who stay in these situations longer than anyone else can understand, they're motivated by irrationalities we all share. Human beings adapted to avoid defeat at all costs, only for society's relationship narratives to become too disordered too quickly for our judgment to catch up. So when we find ourselves experiencing emotional abuse (and between 50 percent and 80 percent of adults have), we choose to savor the scant breadcrumbs of goodness—that pleasant trip to Big Sur two years ago, the nice dinner we had the other month where we didn't fight at all. Clinging to these morsels, we push past the cognitive dissonance, justifying all the acridity, so we don't have to admit to our sunk costs and change.

As time passes, I can see with more clarity that Mr. Backpack was not a monster. I don't believe he got off on causing pain. Equally, I was not a limp sliver of bacon in that relationship. That Mr. Backpack was older and the whole thing was taboo was, I admit, part of my attraction to it. There were flecks of gold between us—our inside jokes, our shared sense of adventure. There had to be, or else I would've never entered the mine in the first place. I never would have stayed. Just like cult survivors.

Sometimes when I confide in a new friend about my experience, they'll ask why my parents didn't try to stop it, and I think, well, their hands were tied. Attempting to control me might've only pushed me away. Just like a parent watching their eighteen-year-old kid run off with a fringe religious group, they hoped I'd get what I needed from it and one day safely come home.

I wouldn't even tell my younger self not to start dating Mr. Backpack. I was a stubborn teenager, so there's no way that advice would've worked. But I also think being too careful in life, too afraid of pain, prevents you from experiencing the most magical parts of it.

What I would say to my teenage self, though, is that no one in history ever transformed from an asshole to a dreamboat just because their girlfriend really wanted them to. I'd tell her that no one expects you to resign yourself forever to a choice you made in high school. I'd tell her it's okay to be "disloyal" to someone who's hurting you. I'd tell her that it is never an unreasonable time to stop and ask of your relationship: Who is this person for whom I'm rewriting my story? Not who were they seven years ago, or who do I hope they'll be, but who are they right now?

The sex and relationships columnist Dan Savage once offered me a kernel of advice about what to tell someone who you know or suspect to be in a toxic relationship. Regrettably, Savage said, there is not some password or flawless synthesis

A TOXIC RELATIONSHIP IS JUST A CULT OF ONE

of logic you can present to get that person to see what you see. But if you want to help, Savage said you can let the person know, even if you haven't spoken to them in a while, that if they ever want to get out—to stay somewhere, or even just chat—you will be there. You won't judge, interrogate, or throw it in their face. You'll just pick up the phone, open the door. If the person is anything like I was, they might not be effusively receptive to this offer; they might scoff and dismiss it. They might even stop talking to you for a while. But they won't forget. So often, a person in either a cult or cultlike relationship doesn't realize that people can see them suffering—that anyone on the outside loves them or cares. That's part of what keeps them in. Even if it seems painfully obvious, sometimes you have to say a thing out loud for it to be real.

So here's me saying it, maybe to the void, maybe to you: Whether you're under the spell of a lover or a leader, it's never too late to cut your losses. At any time, you can unload the heavy pack from your shoulders, leave it on the mountain, and turn back, because the view you were promised isn't actually up there, and it's not worth the climb anymore. It's okay to forgive yourself (after all, everyone has their baggage) and to build a life that's so full, and so yours, that you never really sunk any costs at all.

FOUR

THE SHIT-TALKING HYPOTHESIS
A note on zero-sum bias

It wasn't so much that I chose to work "in beauty," as we phrased it. It was more that the beauty industry—brewed with the aftershocks of the 2008 economic recession and the relentless image-centricity of Los Angeles—stumbled across me and thought yes, fine, you will do.

I'd just graduated college and was pounding the proverbial pavement for nine months in search of full-time employment when I finally landed a salaried writing job . . . penning cosmetics reviews for a women's lifestyle website. I wanted to work at a feminist outlet like *Jezebel*, or perhaps in a newsroom like the *L.A. Times*, or even for a bookish nonprofit. I emailed everywhere. But hunting down entry-level literary positions in L.A. was like whale-watching in Kansas. Meanwhile, the "lipstick effect"—a phenomenon first described during the Great Depression when the general economy was down the tubes, but sales of affordable luxuries like beauty products were way up—had carved a slippery little niche of opportunity. So although I had no idea what a "skincare routine" even was, when an offer to write absolutely anything for money came my way, I wasn't feeling picky.

My first assignment was to drive to Beverly Hills to interview an ocean-eyed movie star about how she healed her rosacea with nothing but lotions from the drugstore, and then pretend to believe her as I reported my findings to a readership of twenty-five- to thirty-four-year-old women cruising the internet on their lunch breaks. Promoting overpriced, unnecessary personal care products to cure a bevy of aesthetic concerns that the industry itself had invented (objectively speaking, wrinkles and cellulite are not "problems") wasn't quite the literary dream I'd envisioned. And yet, as I became enveloped by the insular world of microneedling, microblading, dermaplaning, CoolSculpting, vagina steaming, "vampire facials," "blorange is the new 'it girl' hair color," and Kylie Jenner lip kit drops constituting breaking news, I could only resist its influence so much. Motivated (with great shame) to experience what I never did in high school—the feeling of being a "popular girl," like in the movies—I took it as a social challenge to appear as though I naturally belonged. I couldn't have imagined the bottomless inferno of comparisons I was stepping into. At the time, becoming a "beauty girl" seemed like a lighthearted game I could win.

Within three years, I was practically a cyborg: highlighted, spray-tanned, Botoxed, eyelash-extended, manicured and pedicured, steamed and extracted, Brazilian sugared, Facetuned. I didn't look related to my family. I'd spent two full paychecks on a handbag the size of a greeting card. Every surface of my apartment spilled over with creams, nostrums, and laser-y skincare gizmos, some costing hundreds of dollars apiece, which a parade of overworked public relations ladies had sent me giddily for free, praying I'd publish a paragraph of endorsement. The mid-2010s presented a cultural moment that advocated the most impossible, Kardashian-cum-Glossier-shaped beauty standards of all time; and yet, the era's deluge of quasi-feminist body positivity messaging simultaneously told us that while women should absolutely look like Bratz dolls, they also weren't allowed to complain if they didn't. I felt caught. While I was motivated to keep this job that was so difficult to find, I didn't want to suggest that "beauty" was something anyone *needed*, while at the same time not feeling fully convinced that I didn't need it myself.

I developed a panoply of coping mechanisms to manage the cognitive dissonance. These included a macabre fixation on Sylvia Plath, who also worked in the "women's lifestyle" industry in her twenties for the fashion magazine *Mademoiselle*. Famously preoccupied by aesthetics, Plath coveted Revlon's "Cherries In The Snow" lipstick. Her hair color became the subject of vehement debate. Long after her death, arguments were shared over whether Plath's "true self" was a blonde smiling in a bikini or her "brown haired personality," which she described in a 1954 letter to her mother as "more studious, charming, and earnest." As I applied my bronzer and curled my hair each morning before work, I'd loop the 1988 song "Bell Jar" by the Bangles. *I don't look like this genuinely*, I reassured myself. *I'm playing a character. I'm in drag. Just do the job, and spend every spare moment plotting how to get out. Oh, and try not to put your head in the oven.*

Trickily, though, the difference between pretending to look a certain way and genuinely looking that way is, to say the least, subtle. My experience of life and selfhood became increasingly out of body, especially as Instagram usurped reality. By 2017, Instagram was not just sunsets and brunch porn but an infinite Potemkin village of exotic vacations, trendy unrepeated outfits, and skin the texture of iPhone screens. I was instructed to grow my own "following" in order to represent the website that employed me. This took hours of daily hashtagging, commenting, following, and unfollowing. Every hour, my algorithm introduced me to a new set of accounts I didn't know existed to compare myself to. Despairingly, I felt in my bones that another beauty editor's blonde only made me more brunette, that each influencer's follower count personally rendered me irrelevant. There was a limited quantity of light in the universe, I was sure, and merely learning that someone else was burning bright dimmed me.

This kind of scarcity-minded sorrow is rooted in *zero-sum bias*: the false intuition that another party's gain directly means your loss. Zero-sum bias tells us that if another person is succeeding, then you must be failing. This mentality motivates countless conflicts, from young people's distress about their grades all the way to public resistance to trade and immigration. The puzzle of zero-sum bias is typically discussed in the context of economics, in the pervasive suspicion that a transaction cannot possibly benefit both parties equally. Whenever someone profits from an exchange, we tend to assume that the other guy must have gotten ripped off, even though that's the opposite of how trade actually works, or else no one would do it. "When people try to talk about economics, they have the intuition that the economy as a whole should be a pie we're all sharing—the more you get, the less I have," David Ludden, a language psychologist at Georgia Gwinnett College, explained to me. "But we can actually increase the amount there is in the world to share. Or we can negotiate things to a point where we both benefit."

Unless coerced or outright duped, consumers don't routinely buy things they value less than the price. Equally, vendors do not sell things they value for more. And yet, studies find that the mistaken judgment that they do appears "endemic" in the way humans think about exchange. A 2021 paper published in the *Journal of Experimental Psychology* uncovered a smorgasbord of everyday misbeliefs linked to zero-sum bias, like that the government can't possibly support one group without directly harming another, or that buyers of a good or service are far less likely to benefit from the transaction than sellers. The researchers labeled this fallacious outlook "win-win denial," concluding that among humans, it "may be ubiquitous."

Whether we're talking money or beauty, our zero-sum territorialism is anchored in millennia of stiff resource competition. When small, cloistered communities were our only way of life, another's gain often did mean your loss. Mates, food, and status were effectively finite and not guaranteed to be allocated evenly. "Many things are still like that. If you and I are going to share a plate of pizza, the more you eat the less I get," said Ludden.

Arguably, though, win-win scenarios are the entire reason people accomplish more in groups than they do individually. Discussing "folk economics," anthropologist Pascal Boyer and political scientist Michael Bang Petersen suggested that humans may have adapted for "like-kind exchanges," including barter. Tangible transactions like swapping crops for tools make the mutual benefits of specialization and trade fairly obvious. But there's nothing to suggest those intuitions would carry over to modern-day capitalist dealings involving money, stocks, or heaven forbid, cryptocurrency. Money did not even become globally embraced until after the bartering system faded during the Industrial Revolution, and once the gold standard was abandoned in 1971, the concept of "value" was reduced to an even more puzzling abstraction.

In the Information Age, our understanding of what "currency" and "worth" even mean has warped beyond recognition. When the water is capitalism, a sense of dread that we might not be getting what we're worth is ever present. What "price" can we even assign to our time and creative output to begin with, and what are the chances we'll actually earn that, or that those earnings will feel satisfying? The overthinkers among us (hi) are well positioned to turn our already clunky instincts about money into full-blown paranoias that everyone we trade with for anything—not just cash, but time, clout, or ideas—exists only to deplete us. This wary mistrust is a symptom of burnout, and it can push us to map our dread onto environments that feel more within our control, like our social media feeds.

Sometimes, we hallucinate that an "exchange" is happening at all. How can we expect to gauge our social wins and losses accurately, when a combination of hyper-accessibility and physical detachment has overcomplicated our ability to determine who even constitutes our social circle in the first place? Who am I materially in competition or cooperation with at any given time? Is it just my friends, family, and colleagues? What about colleagues I only know on Slack? Are people who follow me on Instagram in my social circle? Realistically, who are we to each other? These questions are not simple to answer.

We wage our social bets in a very specific way: Our worst "competitors" usually remind us of ourselves. Living in beauty editor land, I never measured myself against men, or women much older than I, or gals who worked in the graphic design department whose "vibes" were so different from mine that it would've been like comparing bananas to blueberries. Instead, the figures that drove me maddest were women my age who had enough in common with me that they posed a threat, or at least they might have twelve thousand years ago. How ironic that the people I might've clicked with best were those who made me want to get rid of all my mirrors and lobotomize myself?

Most acutely, zero-sum bias affects those who've been nurtured by individualist societies, which stress win-lose binaries at every turn. An old friend of mine spent her early childhood in Japan, where attitudes, by Western standards, lend themselves more to collectivism than competition. This friend grew up to become a working actress in New York City, one of the world's most cutthroat professions, where a surplus of dreamers vie for a scant number of roles, and people's appearances really are compared one-to-one. Amid all that, my friend still exudes a sense of calm that has always stupefied me. "In Japan, people don't overthink themselves like they do here," she said once, before telling me about a birthday party she'd just attended in Manhattan for her neighbor's four-year-old daughter. The event dismayed my friend, not only due to the opulent menu, decor, gifts, and attention, but also the downright Olympic intensity of the party games: pin the tail on the donkey, musical chairs, piñatas. All toddling guests were required to participate, and half the "losers"—including the birthday girl herself—wound up in tears. These were preschoolers. "I just thought, if you're going to throw a big ridiculous party, shouldn't it at least be fun?" my friend asked.

In 2017, a sequence of experiments conducted out of the University of Michigan found that students living in East Asian countries were significantly more likely than Westerners to value being a "small fish in a large pond." That is, they would prefer to work a lower-ranking job at a more prestigious company than higher up at a small, no-name firm. Meanwhile, kids who come of age in a society that pushes them to do whatever it takes to capture an enviable title, and not worry who's ravaged along the way, will likely learn to treat all success-geared activities as zero-sum.

Financial stress can also aggravate these deceptions. One 2010 study suggested that Americans either chronically or currently of low socioeconomic status are more likely to jump to zero-sum conclusions. It follows that during times of broader economic strain, public opposition to immigration and trade spikes. During the children's birthday party game from hell that was the 2016 U.S. presidential election, candidates who promoted populist, anti-trade policies enjoyed extraordinary superfandom across the political spectrum, despite criticism from economists. Whether we're discussing hair color or immigration attitudes, the urge to compare even in the face of unlimited resources intensifies when we feel culturally unmoored.

After five years working in the beauty industry, I jubilantly quit with high hopes of making a living reporting on subjects other than eye cream. At long last, I naively presumed, I was emancipated from comparison purgatory. I let my roots grow out. I broke up with my lash artist. I unfollowed all the pouty influencers whose immaculate images had always made me feel dweebish. I was so happy . . . for precisely three weeks. Then my Instagram algorithm figured me out. It could tell I'd shuffled my priorities. Rapidly, my feed adjusted from promoting beauty editors in midi dresses on press trips in Tulum to young Brooklyn-based writers with stern bobs whose debut page-turners had just cracked the *New York Times* bestseller list. This was patently worse. Pitting myself against other women on the internet was a pattern long ago embedded in my system, but now, it wasn't just about looks, it was about my career, my wit, my soul. Before, there was always someone with better highlights and a more glamorous social calendar, wearing off-the-shoulder Dior on a rooftop. Now, there was always someone with flashier bylines, ritzier degrees, and leatherier jackets who didn't wear makeup or even care about social media, and seemed to radiate a bohemian sense of disdain for those who did.

Who was I amid these two extremes? A bad impersonator of each? In short order, I'd go from placidly scrolling to holding my breath as I panic-googled the education and accolades of some hot new writer I'd just discovered. Then, I'd spend a handful of hours mad-scientist-conspiring how I could inflate my value to beat her. Each time, the subject of my fevered fixation was a person who I didn't know walked the earth the day before. She had no effect on my life whatsoever. It was someone I could've even messaged and befriended or collaborated with. Easily, this human and I existing in the world at the same time could be a win-win. Perhaps if I'd only been introduced to her in person—beheld the crinkle of her smile, her nervous fidgets—that would have been more obvious. But the uncanny medium of social media all but destroyed my odds of pushing past zero-sum bias's trickery. I'm ashamed. Ruminating for even thirty seconds on the knowledge that a record of these demented Google benders exists somewhere in the cloud makes me want to pop an Imodium and nap for a year.

Whenever I got hooked into a death helix of comparison, I masochistically found myself hunting for *more* people to compete with. Off I went, seeking out threats as if I were a nomad in the brush, except I was a spoiled cyborg on the internet, and there were endless "enemies" to find. For months, a handful of strangers lived rent-free in my head, and the behaviors I exhibited as a means to exorcise them were as irrational as my anxieties. Frequently, I found myself shit-talking these strangers—both out loud to my friends and silently in my mind—attempting to tease out how I could scoop up more candy from the ghost piñata of my own invention. I wasn't the only one. Many of my peers, especially in creative fields, harbor their own sets of parasocial competitors. When an angel-voiced musician friend showed me the TikTok singer who'd haunted her soul all year, I couldn't believe she'd allowed this strange assortment of pixels to endanger her self-esteem. "Are her songs catchier than mine?" my friend pleaded. "Who even cares?!" I wailed back. "You are so special! Her music has nothing to do with yours!" Embarrassingly, I did not possess the self-reflection to apply this advice to myself.

It was hard not to notice how these zero-sum plights disproportionately affected the women in my life. Where gender and social comparison are concerned, research indicates that women are prone to make more upward comparisons and downward identifications. A 2022 study out of Vaud University of Teacher Education in Switzerland found that by elementary school, girls have already learned to compare themselves only to the peers they perceive as superior. By contrast, when men glance around a party or scroll through their feeds, they're more likely to notice only their less attractive peers. Their impression from there is, *Cool, I guess I'm the hottest guy here*, and that's a self-esteem victory. When women survey their circle, they only spy the "threats."

The consequences are material and stark. A 2022 study from Macquarie University in Australia confirmed a vicious feedback loop of upward social comparison, problematic social media use,* depression, and low self-esteem, disproportionately affecting women. The year prior, a study out of Southwest University in Chongqing, China, determined that teenagers with TikTok use disorder (compulsions to scroll to the point of negative life interferences) suffered heightened

---

* Social media use was considered "problematic" when users logged on despite damaging consequences to their health and relationships. It didn't matter how often they checked their apps; any frequency could be considered problematic.

anxiety, depression, stress, and working memory difficulties. The core features of Instagram and TikTok are precisely what make it so damaging—their addictive nature, perfectionistic filters, algorithmically suggested accounts, and incentives to show only curated highlights set up young women for psychological failure. Users don't take the emotional massacre lying down, but their retaliation isn't pointed at the app itself. Rather, it's directed at other users in the form of shit-talking and subtweeting.

The deception that capitalism and feminism pair well is premium zero-sum bias fuel. In my professional life, I have been swindled under the guise of "partnership" and "mentorship" by more than a handful of women, who were at once victims and perpetrators of the patriarchy's zero-sum game. Following a rulebook that stipulated only a few female players could "win," certain collaborators took the approach of gushing that I reminded them of their younger selves, only to go full Gaslight Gatekeep Girlboss as a means of ensuring I'd never eat their lunch. This category of experience is common, and its consequences are treacherous to all involved. In their 2019 memoir, *Sissy*, author and activist Jacob Tobia discussed how tokenizing marginalized individuals creates a culture of noxious infighting. Tobia wrote, "To sincerely adopt the psychology of tokenism, you have to sell your community out. That's the dark underbelly of the thing. Instead of blaming the institutions, rules, and social attitudes of those around you for the absence of other people like you, you blame your own community."

THE SHIT-TALKING HYPOTHESIS

It may have been in private, but I have spent a truly hideous portion of my precious, mortal life overanalyzing my "competition" in an effort to balance out my insecurity. I've treated the chatter like a hex, aimed at magically transferring the other person's light to me. Temporarily, the catharsis gave me an adrenaline high that felt like it actually might work. But catharsis does not soothe unpleasant feelings—it does the opposite. Freud's catharsis hypothesis endorsed shouting or breaking things in order to "release" negativity, but no modern evidence supports the claim that acting bad is a cure for *feeling* bad. "Given the way the brain works, catharsis does not even make sense. We do not become less likely to [do] something by practicing it," noted a 2013 study on the psychological effects of venting. Snorting a bunch of cocaine never made anyone want to snort *less* cocaine; shit-talking just encourages a person to shit-talk *more*, all the while making them look shady to whoever's listening. Indeed, psychologists have established that when we disparage people behind their backs, something called "spontaneous trait transference" occurs, wherein you start to assume the qualities you're assigning to the subject of discussion. Drone on about your frenemy's bad jokes or tacky sense of style, and sure enough, your fellow conversationalist may start to think of *you* as unfunny and tacky. This finding is consistent; the trouble is that it only applies to in-person interactions. Online, people who talk negatively about others—even if what they're posting is subjective or demonstrably false—are perceived as more in-the-know. More engaging. And thus, algorithmically incentivized to carry on.

It might either comfort or dispirit you to know that no one is impervious to shit-talking in a bid to increase their social value, not even people at the top of their game. Some anecdotal evidence: After the publication of my second book, my partner, Casey, and I were invited to attend a small dinner party hosted by a debut novelist, who'd recently pivoted to literature after enjoying an illustrious career in an '80s rock 'n' roll band. Loose on Pinot Noir, her A-list guests spent the evening trading stories of the zero-sum anxieties shared by their most famous friends. We heard about how Prince always seethed with jealousy of Michael Jackson and that one of the world's most decorated living directors was always insecure that he lacked the edge of his peers. We learned of the day on set when a beloved movie star noticed an issue of a magazine with another scene-stealer on the cover, lifted it above his head, and cursed the sky that his contemporary had achieved such prestige despite only appearing on-screen once every few years.

Channeling every unit of potential energy into keeping my mouth from falling into my lap, I soaked up these stories like a ShamWow cloth. I could have lived a hundred lifetimes and never guessed Prince paid a passing thought to Michael Jackson between churning out his countless bangers. These icons squandered years agonizing over "failures" to stack up to people I'd never think once to compare them to. On the drive home from the party, as Casey and I engaged in the obligatory debrief, he reported to have found these anecdotes discouraging. To me, they were positively liberating. None of us perceives ourself—our attractiveness, our success—accurately. There isn't even one correct way to perceive the same story about someone else's delusion. From my view, if Prince was always self-conscious that he wasn't Michael Jackson, then that meant we're all doomed, and I was free.

Social comparison is instinctive and, at best, it aids in identity formation. No one exits the womb fully equipped with the tools to self-actualize. People have always looked to each other to figure out who the hell they are. As kids, we go to the playground, watch television, or read about people in books and magazines, and we use that information to select qualities we'd like to feature more or less in ourselves. "Well, on Instagram or TikTok, those sources of inspiration come to life 24/7," said psychologist Dr. DiNardo. "Who can resist the urge to go to a playground that's always open?" By DiNardo's account, the manageable way to piece together an identity is by triangulating among a small set of individuals in the physical world. You can't possibly orient yourself amid everyone you see online, especially since the identities presented there are not really people, they're holograms.

Win-win denial, concluded the *Journal of Experimental Psychology*, seems above all else heightened by issues in our theory of mind. As naive realists, human beings can't help but make the perspective-taking error that our own preferences are ground truth. We neglect the fact that everyone we encounter doesn't have the same values or reasoning for their decisions. With respect to economics, the study's authors found that simply reminding participants that buyers and traders have *reasons* for their choices (even shallow ones, like "Mary bought the chocolate bar because she *wanted* it") reduced the prevalence of win-win denial. How easy it is to forget that behind others' real-life choices and social media presences are motivations we could never predict.

While working "in beauty," I was convinced that my contemporaries were Instagramming their lavish Sunset Tower brunches to suck up others' light like a black hole. But maybe it wasn't about that at all. *Mary wanted a photo at brunch that day because it was the first time in months she felt happy. Mary wanted a photo at brunch that day because she thought she looked ugly and wanted to live out a fantasy that she felt beautiful. Mary wanted a photo at brunch that day because her boss told her she needed to post more on Instagram.* What if posting actually made them miserable? "Perhaps we rarely consider what the people we are comparing ourselves to are sacrificing or losing . . . [like] privacy," offered DiNardo. "Also, why is it that the average person with a ton of selfies is a narcissist, but someone 'famous' doing it is amazing? Both people want the same things, no?"

Recognizing that other people can think and feel differently from us is essential for harmonious relationships. Psychologists have noted that this ability is a key developmental step for two- and three-year-old children. It comes with a well-functioning frontal lobe, the part of the brain responsible for reasoning, problem-solving, creativity, communication, and attention. Without flexible, active frontal

THE SHIT-TALKING HYPOTHESIS

lobes, our capacity to see things beyond black and white is compromised. We can't achieve social harmony. In 2023, psychologist Jonathan Haidt argued in *The Atlantic* that smartphones should be banned from schools, citing evidence that teens' constant internet usage destroys their social potential. "If we want children to be present, learn well, make friends, and feel like they belong at school, we should keep smartphones and social media out of the school day for as long as possible," he said. I've wondered: *Has too much time on social media stunted the activity and flexibility of my frontal lobe?*

DiNardo's observations in private practice reveal that the worst social-media-related mental health outcomes, like teen suicide, manifest in clients who don't feel admired by their loved ones or enjoy a rich and dynamic life offline. Since long before TikTok, psychological turmoil has been tied up in one's inability to connect with others. "Today it's widely understood that one of the most important factors in preventing and addressing toxic stress in children is healthy social connection," wrote former U.S. surgeon general Vivek H. Murthy in his 2020 book, *Together*. As life grows increasingly virtual, the torment of zero-sum intuitions may prove tougher to thwart.

Fortunately, though, spontaneous trait transference cuts both ways. Effuse about how creative your new colleague is or how kind your friends, and as long as you mean what you say, you'll notice yourself start to take on shinier qualities. This finding does not support suppressing negative emotions.

Rather, it is an invitation to consider zero-sum bias's role in the vicious cycle of ego and trash talk, as well as the promising notion that this cycle can be broken.

Together with her best friend Aminatou Sow, journalist Ann Friedman coined "Shine Theory" as an actionable solution. In a beloved 2013 piece for *The Cut*, Friedman advised, "When you meet a woman who is intimidatingly witty, stylish, beautiful, and professionally accomplished, *befriend her*. Surrounding yourself with the best people doesn't make you look worse by comparison. It makes you better . . . True confidence is infectious." Building self-esteem improves our treatment of others, because it minimizes the false perception that the mere existence of beautiful, successful, cool people puts our beauty, success, and coolness at risk. It reminds us that their light doesn't dim ours. "If Kelly Rowland can come around to the idea that she shines more (not less) because of her proximity to Beyoncé, there's hope for the rest of us," concluded Friedman.

Half a year after leaving "beauty," I decided to take Friedman's suggestion and experiment with an antidote to those maniacal Instagram spirals. Whenever I came across an account that intimidated me, I began by acknowledging the impulse to get competitive and vomit. Then, instead, I'd tap "Follow." *Give yourself the chance to make a connection, not an enemy*, I'd tell myself. I'd direct-message the account holder a sincere expression of admiration for their work. Much of the time, the multilayered human on the other end thanked me kindly, and when they didn't respond, I typically just forgot about it, as if sending the message was enough to release me. Connection was my catharsis. To say the experiment netted positive would be an undersell. Some of the people I messaged ended up becoming dear, real-life friends. I cannot imagine being enemies with them. With our light combined, we are the Chrysler Building. An undeniable win-win.

FIVE

WHAT IT'S LIKE TO DIE ONLINE
A note on survivorship bias

I met my best friend writing a story about dying girls. She was one who happened to live. Racheli's survival was not, despite the well-meaning sentiments of her subscribers, due to some heavenly "miracle," a karmic "reward," or her emphatic commitment to vegan cuisine. She was not "chosen" to live. But that's the trick with *survivorship bias*, the propensity to focus on positive outcomes while ignoring any accompanying misfortunes. This default framing stains our perceptions—some like colored glass, and others like ink and blood.

In 2017, I wrote an article for *Marie Claire* magazine that peered into a community of severely ill young adults who, in the face of a life-altering diagnosis like cancer, turned to YouTube to vlog their lives and deaths. I was moved to pitch the piece after a playlist of makeup tutorials led me to the video backlog of a strawberry-haired twenty-something named Courtney. In the year since Courtney first posted the eyeshadow lesson at hand, she'd developed a deadly brain tumor. YouTube's "recommended" section introduced me to her as a healthy, apple-cheeked preschool teacher filming beauty how-tos on the side. Then, it beckoned me to watch her get diagnosed with brain cancer; endure radiation and surgery; lose her job, hair, and ability to speak; then finish treatment, enter remission, and gain them all back. The whole story took under an hour.

In the following weeks, pieces of YouTube's chronic illness subculture floated into my purview like balloons. There were dozens more like Courtney, if not hundreds: vloggers mostly in their teens and twenties, who either already had a channel and pivoted to illness content upon their diagnosis or who turned to YouTube explicitly to chronicle their health journeys, from first doctor visits to chemo routines to sometimes very bad news. A few channels reached bona fide celebrity status. One of the first and most celebrated belonged to Talia Joy Castellano, a vivacious thirteen-year-old beauty YouTuber with a buoyant laugh that erupted across the screen like a solar flare. Since the age of seven, Talia had been in treatment for stage 4 neuroblastoma, a progressive tumor of the nervous system. At eleven, she launched her channel, and within two years, she'd gained over 1.4 million subscribers, who cherished her precocious wit and daring makeup looks—Cleopatra-style eyeliner, lipstick the color of orchids—but most of all, her unwavering joie de vivre even at death's front door.

"Talia gave people hope," recalled her older sister Mattia. "To watch this little dying girl have such a positive attitude was captivating. She was just posting makeup videos for fun, but as soon as she started talking about childhood cancer, the channel blew up."

Talia helped clear a path for a thriving generation of chronic illness vloggers. I spoke with Sophia Gall, an ebullient Australian teen with cornflower blue eyes and an infectious glee for online shopping and British pop stars. Sophia started her channel after she was diagnosed with osteosarcoma, a rare bone cancer, at thirteen. Two years later, over 145,000 subscribers watched her enter hospice care. There was also Claire Wineland, a lion-hearted cystic fibrosis patient, known to an audience of almost 200,000 for her raspy laugh and macabre-humored vlogs, like "What It's Like to Be in a Coma" and "Dying 101." Raigda Jeha, a soft-spoken Canadian makeup artist with three children and a sequin smile, was given less than three months to live when she developed stomach cancer at forty-two. For two years, Raigda managed her illness holistically and, at the urging of a friend, began posting uplifting one-takes about her experience to YouTube.

I wanted to understand how video blogging shaped these patients' relationships to their own mortality. How did it feel to witness your body fail and your subscriber count flourish synchronically, like day giving way to night?* Most

---

* Dying can do perverse wonders for your web presence. Despite all her expert beauty tutorials, brain cancer survivor Courtney's top-viewed video is "Update: Talking Is Hard," an aphasiac post-surgery Q&A. With over 5 million views, its thumbnail

portrayals of sick teenagers I'd seen cherry-picked only the "miraculous recoveries"—the terminal cancer sufferer who landed on the news after beating the odds with her chin-up attitude. But I'd never encountered anyone with mettle like these dying girls. There was no triumphant comeback for Sophia, whose lithe frame turned gaunt in the year after our interview, until she lost her ability to walk and passed away in 2018. A few months after that, Claire died by stroke after a double lung transplant at the age of twenty-one. Talia didn't quite make it to her fourteenth birthday, leaving behind a bucket list handwritten in bubble letters for her subscribers to check off in her honor. "#10. Have a huge water balloon fight . . . #22. Say yes to everything for a day . . . #56. Deep clean my room." By chance, though, Racheli lived.

When we first met in person, Racheli was twenty-three, closing in on two years of remission from Hodgkin's lymphoma. She had been diagnosed as a senior in college and started vlogging her experience that same day. "I just whipped out my phone," she remembered. Racheli and I lived two neighborhoods from each other in Los Angeles, and after I turned in my article, she invited me out to a nearby dive bar for craft beers. It'd never occurred to me to befriend a source before, but warm, gregarious Racheli made me wonder why ever that was.

---

image features her grimacing next to her radiation helmet against a sparkly pink backdrop. A year after Courtney was declared cancer-free, her view counts dropped by the thousands. Apparently, we're interested in watching someone in the active process of *dying*. But you can only decline for so long, and as far as one's internet engagement is concerned, remission is as bad for business as death itself.

My mother always told me that when people get sick, they become more extreme versions of themselves. If they're cynical, they become more cynical; if they're polite, they become more polite; if they're funny, they get funnier. An extroverted early education major with glittering green eyes, a sleeve of multicolored tattoos, and a talent for hosting lively Shabbat dinners on a budget, Racheli possessed a contagious lust for life that felt linked to the fact that she'd almost lost it. Midway through our friend date, she proposed migrating to a karaoke bar around the corner, and after three hours of belting early-2000s bubblegum pop hits, our bond was sealed. Less than six months later, I sat front row at her wedding. Equally skilled in both crisis and celebration, Racheli became the first person I'd telephone with news of any kind. My parents began inviting her and her husband to all our family gatherings, having forgotten that we didn't grow up together—that months before Racheli knew I existed, I watched her shave her head, flaunt her freshly inserted port, contend with blood clots in her lungs, clang the bell for her last round of chemo, beam in the glow of cake light on her first birthday post-cancer, sigh with relief at the declaration of clean scans, share her hair-growth routine, go back to school, and get engaged . . . all online.

She was a natural on camera, though internet attention was never Racheli's aim. After her diagnosis, she saw YouTube simply as a convenient way to keep her friends and family updated on her health. With any hope, her vlogs might even reach a few other young people with cancer, giving them something to relate to. Racheli's first video opens with a shot of her face like a disco ball, dizzy and bathed in neon strobes. A cheerful electronic song thumps in the background. "So I'm bowling with friends. . . . Today was the day I found out that I have Hodgkin's lymphoma," she tells the lens through a bewildered smile. "I'm a little bit in shock, but I have the most amazing friends." The rest of her video cuts to clips of her running errands with her wide-eyed young pals, starting a new raw food diet, driving to the airport to catch a flight back home to Florida so she could meet with a hematologist there. The vlog, titled "The Day After My Diagnosis with Cancer," ends with an image of Racheli snuggling under lilac bed sheets with a friend. "Everything's gonna be okay," she proclaims.

That line would become Racheli's signature vlog outro. While in treatment, she regarded radical optimism—"using positivity to overcome adversity," she always said—as her survival strategy. But a few years into remission, she started to feel torn about painting her "cancer journey" with such a rosy palette. "Surviving cancer is almost as much of an emotional roller coaster as getting diagnosed," she confessed one evening four months into our friendship, as we sat on her couch in L.A., noshing on Moroccan sfenj she made from scratch. "There's gratitude and PTSD and some anxiety about what other people project onto my experience." Not uncommonly, strangers implied that Racheli's survival was a kind of reward for being someone the world couldn't stand to lose. "First of all, that's so much pressure," she said. "But I know amazing people who did everything 'right' and passed away, and I know awful people who did things 'wrong' and lived. I think some viewers want to think that I survived because I was a positive person, maybe so that they could follow in my footsteps if they ever got sick themselves."

This psychological reconfiguration is the work of survivorship bias. It's an error that shows up not only in life-or-death scenarios, but anywhere "success" is measured: business, fitness, fine art, war. Survivorship bias beckons thinkers to draw incorrect conclusions about "why" something turned out well by fixating too narrowly on the people or objects that made it past a certain benchmark, while overlooking those that didn't.

The canonical survivorship bias example comes from World War II. It was 1943 when the American military solicited Columbia University's statistics team to help them figure out what kind of armor would prevent their fighter planes from getting shot out of the sky. They couldn't outfit an entire aircraft in a knight's shining suit or it would weigh the thing down, so they had to zero in on the most vulnerable areas. The military's intuitive approach was to examine the planes returning from battle and analyze which parts had suffered the greatest damage. Naturally, then, they'd give those areas extra padding. But one of the mathematicians noticed a key flaw in their plan: They weren't thinking about the planes that *hadn't* flown home. Survivorship bias pointed the officers in exactly the wrong direction—to protect against the aircraft injuries that expressly weren't fatal.

The military had no idea which bullet holes hit the worst, because those planes never came back.

This disregard of invisible failures skews our judgment in so many areas of modern life. It emerges when we selectively pay attention to some new workout program's wondrous before-and-afters without considering all the exercisers who wound up with nothing but an uncancelable gym membership and dinged self-esteem. It's when we attempt to copy the exact career path of one role model because it panned out famously for them, even though the same strategy might've flopped for a hundred others we never see. It shows up when we meander through a museum, admiring the craftsmanship of all those ancient Egyptian builders and Victorian seamstresses, deciding they just don't make things like they used to. Meanwhile, we neglect to account for all the bygone clothes, artworks, and edifices that weren't beautiful or masterful enough to keep around. They definitely do make things like they used to—many more of them, in fact. There's just an excess of garbage in the mix as well. For every brand-new, breathtaking bodice made by hand, there is a landfill of flimsy, factory-made message tees. By contrast, all that's left from the "good old days" are their highest-quality products, and thus, that's all we ever see.

One Tabasco-hot summer in Los Angeles, Casey and I ate magic mushrooms and paid a visit to the Getty Museum. Built in the late 1990s, the Getty Center's architecture resembles a city from the distant future. Geometric buildings the color of bone and serpentine gardens spring out of Malibu's dry, auburn mountains like flags on the moon. We'd heard there was a beguiling "Myths of the Middle Ages" exhibit worth visiting and thought a pinch of psilocybin would pair well. Moseying through the displays of ornate apothecary vessels and Middle English scrolls, I was gobsmacked by the artistry of everyone in the 1400s. Then I remembered, this museum didn't represent *everyone*. In fact, half the pieces on display weren't even genuinely medieval—the point of the exhibit was to spotlight romantic reimaginings of the Middle Ages from later years, as craftsmanship became more sophisticated, not less. As one velvet-walled exhibit gave way to a marble atrium, I was struck with wistfulness for the millions of objects that hadn't made it into these galleries because they simply weren't preservation material. You never see the shoddy crafts of bored fifteenth-century teenagers or amateur painters, because they either weren't sturdy or special enough to last. Gawking at an exquisite six-hundred-year-old storybook that belonged to a king, I wondered what itchy wool cloaks and out-of-tune gemshorn flutes my own great-great-great-great-great-grandparents might have made. I thought of how much those mediocre relics might mean to me if they'd managed to survive, even if they weren't objectively worth placing behind reflection-control glass.

Of the six dying girls I interviewed, only one besides Racheli survived. Her name was Mary. She was diagnosed with Ewing's sarcoma, a childhood bone cancer, at age fifteen. I still keep up with Mary on Instagram, and it's by far my most positive use of the app. My heart climbs to my throat every time I see her reach any life milestone, big or small: high school graduation, college acceptance, a new hair color. Her hair came back like an avalanche. When I interviewed Mary in 2017, she had recently finished her last of fourteen chemo rounds. Fuzz had begun returning to her scalp in tawny patches, like continents on a milky globe. Mary was still a minor when she went through treatment, so the decisions about her health weren't entirely up to her. Filming and editing YouTube videos—"A Week with a Cancer Patient | hospital vlog," "Best & Worst Parts of Having Cancer"—became a pleasurable way of gaining some agency. And the sense of routine helped pass those long, boring hospital stays. "When I got sick I was really lonely and didn't have a lot of ways to reach out to people," Mary explained. "YouTube was therapeutic. Even though there were so many terrible things happening, I could make the terrible things into a video, into art. I could share it with people in my own way. That helped me cope." Almost every day, viewers left comments that Mary's videos put their problems into perspective: breakups, bad report cards. "When you see somebody whose battle is so over-the-top, so beyond what you've experienced, you realize that you can get through your own struggles," she said.

As uncanny as it is to grow deeply attached to someone and then mourn their death without ever knowing them in person, mental health experts agree that it's a healthier use of social media than most. Witnessing the daily trials, celebrations, and loss of a young stranger forces followers to look beyond their own circumstances. "Many girls worry about a bad hair day," said Dr. Peg O'Connor, a behavioral health scholar and professor at Gustavus Adolphus College in Minnesota. "But there's a huge difference between a bad hair day because your bangs are too long and a bad hair day because clumps are falling out."

In the way that only the most exceptional physical art pieces from generations past remain, social media users typically preserve only the glossiest exhibitions of their lives. The dying girls' "imperfect" vlogs made use of YouTube as a virtual gallery space, challenging survivorship bias like physical art never could. Their raw, self-authored sketches of day-to-day illness were digital artifacts—a collection of amateur pottery and fabric that can't disintegrate with age.

These young women's videos also questioned the fantasy portrayals of cancer preferred by the news, which only inflame viewers' survivorship bias. "Inspiration porn" defines a whole media genre where folks with severe health impairments are depicted trouncing obstacles with sheer will. Most Americans with disabilities are not sufficiently employed or supported, no matter how resolute they are. A 2015 study published in the *Disability and Health Journal* concluded that individuals with physical disabilities are 75 percent less likely to have their medical needs met than their able-bodied peers. "People with disabilities have largely been unrecognized as a population for public health attention," concluded another 2015 study from the *American Journal of Public Health*. The findings showed that adults with congenital defects, late-onset illness, or injuries were almost three times as likely to be unemployed and more than twice as likely to have a household income of less than $15,000. Most terminal cancer patients don't make "miraculous" recoveries thanks to their swell attitudes. Most dying girls don't become YouTube famous.

When my mother got sick and the dialect of cancer entered my lexicon, I was struck by how naturally people slipped into the language of success and failure to describe life and death. "Losing" one's "battle" with cancer was a chosen forfeiture; it was "giving up," "surrendering." Implicitly, the lesson was to hoard life like gold, and those who "win" it must have deserved it.

Even beyond the domains of disability and death, survivorship bias can create crushing success-failure binaries. Consider the legends of tech CEOs who dropped out of college to become billionaires. So smitten is the zeitgeist with wealthy dropouts that in 2011, tech billionaire and right-wing contrarian Peter Thiel launched a program awarding $100,000 to young entrepreneurs who planned to ditch college. Odds-defying narratives may be sparkly, but they falsely imply that with adequate skill and effort, riches are available to anyone, and if you fail, you're the pitiful exception rather than the invisible norm. Much more common are the untold stories of those with commensurate skills and determination, but whose businesses never took off due to factors beyond their control—lack of family wealth and connections, systemic prejudice, bad timing. In 2017, *Forbes* found that 84 percent of America's top billionaires graduated from college, most earning degrees from Harvard, MIT, or Stanford. These .000001 percenters were more likely to have a master's or PhD than no degree at all.

Forget billionaires. Focusing on portraits of millennials who "made it" in everyday ways—buying property, vacationing in Iceland that one summer when it seemed like *everyone* was in Reykjavík—distorts the reality that the average millennial experience is not so plentiful. According to Pew Research and Federal Reserve data, millennials are more likely to live in poverty than Gen Xers and baby boomers at similar ages. In 2022, the Federal Reserve reported that 31 percent of American millennials and 36 percent of Gen Zers were drowning in student loan debt, which more than doubled between 2009 and 2019. Meanwhile, the internet suggests all young people care about is designer sweatpants and tinned fish. Maybe some spend $16 on trendily packaged anchovies because they know they'll never get out of the red, so what does it matter anyway?

At its roots, survivorship bias is like proportionality bias in that it's powered by a fundamental misunderstanding of cause and effect. Similar to the misjudgments that inspire conspiracy theories, survivorship bias encourages thinkers to read positive causation into patterns where only correlation exists. When Racheli's YouTube commenters saw the heartening twinkle in her eye, survivorship bias convinced them a sunshiny mindset was surely what saved her. This craving to transform senseless misfortune into a logical narrative was part of what motivated Racheli, Sophia, Mary, and Claire to launch their YouTube channels to begin with. Amid the whirlpool of reactions that comes with a grave medical diagnosis is the agony that your life is happening at random, and there's nothing you can do about it. The first time we spoke, Racheli said that the ability to upload YouTube videos and impact her subscribers for the better made the experience feel less meaningless.

"It helped me feel like the hard times were counting for something," she said, "that they weren't just happening for no reason."

We often want real human lives to feel like well-plotted films. We desire obstacles and drama and, ultimately, an ending that blooms from the bulbs planted. I've heard screenwriters discuss the benefits of "but/therefore" storytelling versus "and then" storytelling. Bad movie scripts tack random event onto random event ("and then, and then, and then"). This amounts to an unfulfilling story that doesn't quite track. By contrast, compelling scripts plant narrative seeds, then create conflicts and resolutions that sprout accordingly ("therefore," "therefore," "but," "therefore"). We crave this structure in ourselves as much as we do in fiction.

Life is not a screenplay, but YouTube falls somewhere in between. Video blogs blur the lines between real experience and storytelling, celebrity and sick teenager, audience and friend. When events do not unfold in a fashion that "tracks," some viewers get agitated and lash out. The majority of the feedback Racheli, Mary, Sophia, and Claire received on their videos was supportive, but it was hard not to zoom in on the sparse hostility. Even those facing the unthinkable, who've been forced to rise above the "small stuff," are not immune to the distress of internet malice. Fifteen-year-old Sophia Gall said she got a few comments accusing her of faking her illness and demanding that she be thrown in jail. "I wish that were the truth," she laughed dolefully.

In her forties, Raigda Jeha was part of a smaller faction of Gen X vloggers who didn't grow up with screens. In contrast to Mary's highly curated short films and Racheli's action-packed vlogs, Raigda's videos were typically shot in one take. Seated, her phone held selfie-style, she chatted familiarly about what foods and treatments had been agreeing with her lately. She advised viewers to take an active role in their own care, a palliative approach, encouraging them to weigh their doctors' advice against their own happiness. After posting her first video, Raigda remembered a guy asking why she even bothered putting on makeup if she was dying. "And then you get the trolls saying, 'I have a cure! Buy this!'" she described. "Or people getting upset with me for pushing alternative medicine, which I'm not. There is no cure for me. I'm just sharing my life while I still have it."

In service of balanced expectations, quantitative studies have noted a correlation between optimism and good health. A hopeful disposition is connected to lower levels of depression in depressive patients, decreased risk for heart attack and stroke, and generally longer lifespans. When you begin a new workout routine and proceed to focus solely on its benefits, that technically may be a biased interpretation of results; however, a 2019 study found that participants with the highest levels of "irrational" optimism lived 11 percent to 15 percent longer than those who had no positive thinking practice.

Hope can only aid a body so much, of course. As Siddhartha Mukherjee, author of *The Emperor of All Maladies*, once put it, "In a spiritual sense, a positive attitude may help you get through chemotherapy and surgery and radiation and what have you. But a positive mental attitude does not cure cancer—any more than a negative mental attitude causes cancer." For Talia, Raigda, Sophia, and Claire, a blithe temperament did not "earn" them recovery. And yet, short as their lives were, I was in awe of how they enjoyed them. Shouldn't pleasure alone count as "success," even if it can't be measured the same way?

New York City therapist and mental health educator Minaa B. echoes that longevity aside, developing an optimism practice is worthwhile. "Lacking optimism is largely an issue of lacking personal agency," she told me. "It's when we want life to feel different, but we wake up and do the same thing over and over again. We're not planning, creating, pausing and saying, 'I'm going to take control.'" There's a coziness to inertia even when it's miserable, because the brain knows what to expect. Trying something new, like starting a YouTube channel when you have a serious illness, comes with uncertainty; but, it also yields the very rewards that inspire hope. "Everybody on this earth has responsibilities and hardships, but creating optimism means creating pleasurable changes that flow with those day-to-day responsibilities, so we can feel meaning and purpose," said Minaa B. There will always be erratic "and then" curveballs that threaten our contentment. Ask, then, said Minaa, "How can I make life more pleasurable within my locus of control?"

A few months after Raigda's passing, her daughter uploaded a memorial video to her channel. Its caption read, "She looked forward to making videos for you guys everyday and inspiring everyone. You all gave her hope and something to look forward to every morning. . . . Her death doesn't mean you should lose hope, it should teach you that no matter what obstacles come your way . . . know that pain is temporary . . . and be grateful."

With YouTube, Raigda, Talia, Sophia, and Claire showed that death was real—that "miracles" aren't the only evidence worth reporting. They made visible the dropouts who don't become billionaires and the aircrafts that never fly home. They not only cataloged but humanized and dignified the data we never see. In a sense, YouTube also allowed them to cheat death. "I've got a large family, and these videos are something I can leave behind," Raigda told me three months before her passing, her dulcet voice a wren's closing birdsong. In choosing to document their last days on their own terms, the dying girls could dance with mortality, rather than letting it destroy them. And once their creating days were done, their family and followers could go back at any time and watch their hundreds of vlogs, as if they were still here, tapping sparkles onto their eyelids.

SIX

TIME TO SPIRAL
A note on the recency illusion

For a brief but invigorating flash, I think the aliens really might nuke us once and for all. It's an uncharacteristically sticky evening in Los Angeles—the kind of dense, marshy air on which it's easy to project some kind of sinister meaning—when, hovering like twin flying saucers over the insomniac glow of my laptop screen, the love of my life and I hold our breath as a former army intelligence officer warns America that yes, UFOs are real, and yes, they could come for us any day now.

The date is May 16, 2021, and while Casey and I are situated cozily at home, "home" may not belong to us for much longer. Or so says the latest upload to *60 Minutes*' YouTube channel.

"We have tackled many strange stories on *60 Minutes*, but perhaps none like this," opens a mustached CBS correspondent, his telejournalist's lilt dilating the gravity in the room. "It's the story of the U.S. government's grudging acknowledgment of Unidentified Aerial Phenomena, *UAP*, more commonly known as UFOs."

Eyes wide as Saturn's rings, Casey and I ensconce ourselves on the couch in the dark, as the correspondent squints at his panel of firsthand UAP witnesses—a handful of ex-navy pilots and air force officers—scanning for delusion. One foggy-eyed former lieutenant with a shaved scalp recounts a fleet of mysterious hovercrafts whirring at inexplicable speeds through both air and water off the coast of Virginia "every day for at least the past couple of years." The correspondent interrupts, "Wait a minute, every day for a couple of *years*??" Resigned, the lieutenant nods: *"Mhmm."*

On a loop, *60 Minutes* replays the same black-and-white video clips captured grainily by infrared military cameras: a fuzzy charcoal fleck glides across the frame like an animatronic housefly. An iridescent isosceles slips through the atmosphere, flickering like a lighthouse . . . or a tracking device? Some of this footage is decades old, but it's making airwaves now, thanks to a congressional order that the Pentagon release the unclassified UAP documents they've apparently been hiding since the 1980s. Starting next month, the report will be made available for anyone to peruse online as conveniently as a Reddit thread. These UAP are now officially considered a "national security risk," the ex-CIA chap tells CBS, and it's high time the public knew.

Casey and I watch a lot of space videos together. Little internet films about Fermi's paradox, or terraforming the moon, or how the largest galaxy supercluster in the observable universe compares in size to the smallest quark. We've been together for five years but have known each other since childhood, an age when aliens, dinosaurs, and the tooth fairy all seemed equally plausible. Casey and I went to performing arts school together in Baltimore and reconnected a decade later in L.A. He came here to compose music for movies and video games—I've overheard him in the other room scoring sci-fi scenes not unlike the one we're watching now. Learning about black holes and light-years feels like therapy to us, two sensitive teenagers turned overthinking adults, who need regular reminders of how puny we are. Sometimes I wonder if that's why people in L.A. can be so self-centered: The narcissism isn't innate, there's just too much light pollution to see the stars.

We always check the comments. About a minute into the UAP video, Casey and I scroll down to gauge how this decidedly retro threat of alien invasion is sitting with the masses. He suggests the unidentifiables might be secret Russian technology, if anything. "I hope it's aliens, and I hope they beam me up first," I half joke, though my honest inkling is that they're nothing more than an optical illusion—light and color, deceiving us somewhere between the part of the mind that sees and the part that judges. Growing up, I had a book of classic illusions that mesmerized me for hours on end: pages of visual mind-trickery, like the Rubin vase (that ambiguous Rorschach-esque image that either looks like a goblet or a pair of faces), impossible objects (staircases that somehow ascend forever, cubes that don't connect on the logical axes), and stills of mottled shapes that seem to pulse or rotate due to peripheral drift, a glitch in our pattern detection system. Some say a cognitive bias is a "social illusion." Our minds always fill in gaps to tell a story—the one at hand, a tale of space-age wonder. "This is nuts lol. The world changes so fast right in front of our very eyes," reads the UAP video's top comment. The remark receives a total of seventeen thousand likes.

That a swarm of technologically hyper-advanced extraterrestrials had arrived to surveil and possibly torch our humble planet was hardly the most dystopian concern the American news media assigned our frayed little nervous systems in 2021, but it was up there. Amid the global pandemic, the ever-escalating climate crisis, and famines the world over, there was already so much to pay attention to. Too many Armageddons for our sweet Stone Age amygdalas to process. Empirically, not every headline that successfully pulled focus even qualified as "news," much less urgent news, but panicking usually felt like the safest response anyway, at least to me. Not to brag, but I am phenomenal at freaking out for little to no reason. Ask Casey, who has to deal with overhearing constant dramatic gasps from across the house day after day. It's weird, during moments of actual crisis (I coached us through a bear encounter while camping a few years back), I run oddly calm. But if my YouTube algorithm suggests a twelve-year-old TED Talk about earthquake preparedness or why American funeral practices are poisoning the soil—never mind that it's a harmless collection of pixels, the video's outdated subject matter no immediate threat—my body eagerly spirals without my mind's permission.

Turns out, this objectively nonsensical style of panic sprouts from a deep-rooted cognitive bias called the *recency illusion*—the tendency to assume that something is objectively new, and thus threatening, simply because it's new to you.* Anyone who's ever responded to an abstract, nonurgent "peril" as if it were about to push them off a cliff can thank this ever-present fallacy, which dupes us into believing that a thing only just happened because you only just happened to notice it—even if it's actually been there for hours, months, or thousands of years.

Coined in 2007 by Stanford linguist Arnold Zwicky, the recency illusion was first observed in language. It describes the impulse to react to a word or grammatical construction you've never heard before by deducing it naturally must be some deviant form of slang, which entered the lexicon only

---

* YouTube has a whole category explicitly targeting the recency illusion: A bespoke homepage playlist titled "New to *You*" suggests three-, five-, twelve-year-old videos it knows you haven't seen. The day of this writing, my "New to You" section includes news coverage of a volcanic eruption from three years ago, an eleven-month-old astrophysics explainer on whether or not there are other dimensions, and a 2013 *Vice* offering titled "Westminster Dog Show . . . on Acid!" Predictably, I clicked them all.

recently and ergo poses a threat to English, like a tuft of crabgrass sullying a pristine lawn. The recency illusion explains many of the misconceptions I encountered in my earlier writing about feminist sociolinguistics. Like when people would get terribly bent out of shape over the blasphemous new idea of using "they" as a singular pronoun, despite the fact this usage can be found in writings as old as the fourteenth century. (Chaucer, Shakespeare, and Austen were all fans of singular "they.") Or how folks would huff and puff about the downright godless use of "literally" to mean "not literally," even though this definition has existed for 250 years.*

There was something special about the UFO story's effect on the modern mind. For that one week in May, everyone I knew clung to it like lint to a warm sock. An alien attack—it was such a refreshingly unifying fear. Politics felt outright petty in comparison. You have so many enemies on earth until conflicts turn intergalactic. Confronted with an army of hypersonic hovercrafts, even Mitch McConnell starts to look like a quasi-friendly face. A celestial invasion also felt just plain whimsical. Unlike the era's other existential

---

* It's not abnormal for words to come to mean their precise opposites. Depending on the context, "literally" can mean "virtually" or "in effect," and dictionaries have long approved of this additional definition. The second entry for "literally" in Merriam-Webster's reads: "used in an exaggerated way to emphasize a statement or description that is not *literally* true or possible." When a single word has two definitions that counter each other, that's called a "contronym," and there are dozens of them in English, including the word "fine" (which can either mean really nice or just adequate), "transparent" (which can either mean invisible or obvious), or the use of "bad" to mean "good" (as in, "Omg, you are *baaaaad*").

perils—starvation, disease—at least it lent itself to imagination: What did the aliens look like? What part of the universe had they come from? Were they here to study us? Or save us? Or were we comparatively so primitive that after scanning our cute cerulean sphere, they quickly determined there was no intelligent life to speak of and were planning any day now to zap our resources, like chopping down a tree for the scrap wood with little pity for its squirrel tenants, and continue on their merry way? Sensible or not, I welcomed this space-themed version of doom. Finally, I thought, a cataclysm we could all agree to fixate on for a while. That was wishful thinking, of course, and to my disenchantment, by the following week, no one cared about UAP anymore. Headlines had moved on to supply chain shortages and a TikTok-famous sheepadoodle named Bunny, and so had the clicks and ad dollars. But for what felt like a longer than average stretch of time, our collective attention was tethered to the stars.

Watching *60 Minutes* with Casey that swampy L.A. night felt like a riddle. Was it not a strange coincidence that these skybound enigmas just so happened to show up and become a "national security risk" the moment we just so happened to invent the technology to notice them? Scrolling through all the frazzle and conspiracy in the YouTube comments, I was desperate to understand what made the Pentagon's reports feel so threatening, when it seemed that even in the wild unlikelihood that these UAP really were super-sophisticated aliens, they probably would have gotten here millennia ago. And if they hadn't caused us harm yet, it's not like we had any indication that they'd start. What about the human mind convinces us that a piece of novel information is worthy of panic, and then, just as perplexing, what makes us so quickly forget and move on? When figures with media power treat an event as new and inherently dangerous even when it isn't, are they purposefully fear-mongering for profit? Or does some even stronger force have a hold on them, too?

Whenever a mysterious human behavior inspires the question, "Why are we like this?"—and the longer I live, the more those seem to come up—the psychological explanation is often one of two things: Either the irrationality at hand carries a slightly outdated evolutionary benefit (a cognitive wisdom tooth, if you will), or it's merely an inconvenient side effect of some other legitimately useful trait (scientists sometimes call this a "spandrel"; the human chin is a physical example).* Other times the source of a cognitive bias is frustratingly unclear, but in the case of the recency illusion, it's likely the former.

After inhaling the UFO video, I found myself on a lurid Google bender that led me to an article enumerating the #1 cause of death at different points throughout human history. Until the advent of agriculture, anthropologists' best guess is that most people who made it past childhood perished from

---

* Humans are the only living species that have chins. As diets changed over the millennia, our jawbones and muscles got more compact, but they left behind an odd piece of bone protruding from the bottom of our faces—the chin—which itself serves no clear purpose. Now go ahead and picture a cat with a chin. It's weird.

external causes, like falls, drowning, and animal attacks. When sudden, avoidable injuries were the leading source of danger, it paid to be on high alert for sudden, avoidable threats. Whether a predator rustling in the bushes was truly new or just new to you was trifling minutiae. Our attention was limited, and fresh input naturally claimed it every time. "Recency is linked to relevance, right? We think of something recent as more salient," Sekoul Krastev, co-founder of the behavioral economics research firm The Decision Lab, explained to me in an interview.

Human attention is still bounded, but as modern stimuli are typically more conceptual than movement in the bushes, it's harder to know where to point our focus, what's genuinely worthy of our distress. In her book *How to Do Nothing: Resisting the Attention Economy*, artist and technology critic Jenny Odell articulated the driving relationship among attention span, speed, and low-quality news. She lamented that the capitalistic pressure to "colonize the self," to treat our bodies and minds like productivity machines, is identical to that which colonizes our time with excess news. "Those same means by which we give over our hours and days [to work] are the same with which we assault ourselves with information and misinformation, at a rate that is frankly inhumane," wrote Odell.

Blending digital news with the recency illusion makes for a potent hallucinogen. How swiftly this two-ingredient elixir distorts our ability to discern what input is novel versus out-of-date, relevant or dismissible, menacing or safe. Once attention itself became a form of currency, online media outlets were incentivized to frame every event as urgent and hazardous as a way to compete for it. For the five years I worked as an online beauty editor, my assignment was to churn out six daily articles that could capture the type of viral engagement of *60 Minutes*'s alien video. Every day, my team of editors was assigned to repromote old stories, refreshing nothing but the headlines to make them seem mission-critical: "9 Bloat-Causing Diet Mistakes Nutritionists Want You to Stop Making *Yesterday*," "This Kendall Jenner–Approved Foundation Is Suddenly Flying Off Shelves," "Could This Buzzy New Skincare Ingredient Secretly Give You Buttne?"* We'd audience-test to determine which article titles and newsletter subject lines produced the best click-through rate. (Odd numbers performed better than evens; Kardashians were out, Jenners were in. These strategies now seem fully prehistoric, compared to the AI and neuromarketing tools waiting in the wings.) Squeezing every clickbait structure into one headline became a demented game. We editors weren't exploiting readers' nervous systems on purpose. We didn't know the neuroscience. But the implicit understanding in that office was that if a problem felt new, it'd feel more serious, and if it felt more serious, it'd likely provoke onlookers' interest, generating more traffic and revenue for our bosses, and allowing us to keep our jobs. The stakes of beauty journalism are comparatively low, but hard-hitting newsrooms

---

* You know, buttne. Like acne, on your butt.

are incentivized to generate traffic this same way. Consider the CIA's choice to update UFOs to UAP. That wasn't motivated by accuracy alone—it, too, was a headline refresh.

Headlines and thumbnails wield a physiological power. They work to hijack our amygdalas, the tiny kidney-bean-shaped region of the brain's limbic system, its emotional headquarters. Some psychologists nickname the amygdala our cognitive "alarm system." When the area receives a signal indicating either peril or opportunity, it unleashes a gush of hormones, which causes us to feel specific bodily sensations (butterflies, queasiness). Instantly, these sensations affect the direction of our focus, informing almost every unconscious thing we do: our argument styles, our crushes, the shape and size of our search engine sprees. The brain's emotional headquarters is much older and more primitive than its rationality department, the prefrontal cortex. The limbic system has been around since human beings' only two significant concerns were to find food and avoid becoming it. Over the millennia, our sympathetic nervous systems grew expertly good at assuming the worst. After all, there was no upside to "rationalizing" yourself out of overreacting to a stimulus. The stakes were too high. In noble pursuit of keeping us alive, our emotional brain has "first dibs" on interpreting incoming information. While the prefrontal cortex is well equipped to sort through complex datasets before arriving at a conclusion, it only has second dibs, and the amygdala prefers to get there via cognitive pole vault. Struggling to tell the difference between steep cliffs and clickbait, our stress hormones respond to both with the same fights, flights, and freezes—reactions which, in the digital age, have become both valuable and targeted.

If clickbait is the trigger that sets off our cognitive alarm systems, news algorithms are the anarchists pulling it. You are presented with an initial signal—Apple News floats a UAP article into your inbox—and if you engage with that piece of news, you're of course likely to see exponentially more of the same. In real time, a series of both true and false alarms is personalized to your limbic system, so soon enough, all you can talk about is UAP or buttne or the hazards of figurative "literally." The content may not truly be new, but your mind reacts to the stress of viewing it as hastily as it would to a noise in the brush. Writing for online magazines, I saw how this sausage was made, and even so, I scarfed it down with alacrity. The digital media industry could not exist without the recency illusion, and while much of the alarmism is manufactured with profit and perniciousness, this bias spares no one. I've watched media higher-ups read their own headlines and flip out. No one fretted more over bloat and buttne than that beauty website's CEO.

For a few moments in May of 2021, seventeen thousand YouTube users, including me, beheld a bunch of flying saucers careening across a screen and felt in our bones that the world was changing "right in front of our very eyes." But then, the world didn't change . . . at least not enough to keep our stress hormones flowing and focused on UAP. As soon as we determined the coast was clear with regard to aliens—no crop circles, no abductions—we moved on.* In a news cycle that sheds and regrows its skin every hour, our attention is perpetually straying from events that have lost their flashiness in order to accommodate the latest potential disaster, even if the new one is objectively less salient than the threat that came before it.

A memory: Five years before the UAP news, in the summer of 2016, the day-to-day lives of everyone I cared about revolved around protests and fundraising in the wake of the Pulse nightclub tragedy, the mass shooting at an LGBTQ+ nightclub in Orlando, Florida. But come autumn, those waves of intense, guttural outrage seemed to have crested and fallen. My social media feeds went from clamorous anti–gun violence resources and professions of fury back to pouty selfies and brunch pics. I, too, was flummoxed by my own behavior. Why *wasn't* I shouting at the top of my lungs about the Second Amendment anymore?

Brain scientists agree these shifts are not always due to a lack of care. As decision researcher Sekoul Krastev explained, "The issues brought to light during social reckonings like #MeToo and Black Lives Matter all already existed, and the reactions to them were in a sense long overdue. But the thing

---

* The hormonal rewards of constantly checking our phones fatigue the mind just as much as the stressors do. Studies of phone addiction have found that the little hits of dopamine that keep users jonesing for notifications come with a tragic side effect—they actually inhibit the amount of dopamine we feel when exposed to real-life novelty. Said another way, phone addiction decreases our ability to enjoy new experiences in the physical world. When you're hooked on novelty in electronic form, new foods and flowers lose their magic.

is, the same power that gave those issues salience gave other things salience very quickly thereafter." Our nervous systems struggle to sustain agitation for the many crises news platforms serve us, especially when material changes don't result right away. "The brain is not prepared to be exposed to trauma so very often. It also needs positive feedback to help us step out of survival mode," added psychotherapist Minaa B. Cognitive biases like the recency illusion encourage us to see the world through a black-and-white, life-or-death filter. "But if we can't honor the fact that life isn't either *all* panic or *all* contentment, then that just exacerbates feelings of anxiety and depression. It isn't helpful. We need to honor that multiple truths can exist at once," said Minaa.

A 2019 study by scientists at the Technical University of Denmark suggested that over the last century, the sheer quantity of knowable information has caused the global attention span to shrink. "It seems that the allocated attention time in our collective minds has a certain size but the cultural items competing for that attention have become more densely packed," commented Sune Lehmann, one of the study's authors. This cognitive exhaustion, paired with our attraction to newness, causes us to flip-flop between topics at quickening intervals. From the recency illusion's perspective, after an initial rush of pressure, people tend to let go of an issue as quickly as they embraced it. Of course, some don't have the privilege of redirecting their attention to the most au courant problem, because the previous one is still an active emergency for them. Not simply to survive but to make the best of our ever-complicating world, we have to remember: When assessing the salience of contemporary concerns, we can't always trust our attention as the most reliable barometer.

There is never enough time or meaning, and our most dizzying cognitive biases concern the maximization of both. Business leaders have tried coming up with schemas for how to reconcile the two in the workplace, like the late Peter Drucker, who published a few dozen books over the course of his life on time management. "Efficiency is doing things right; effectiveness is doing the right things," Drucker wrote in 1966's *The Effective Executive*. "There is nothing quite so useless as doing with great efficiency something that should not be done at all." One of Drucker's signature techniques was to create an urgent-vs.-important matrix, which could also be labeled a "time-meaning matrix." A professional task is not necessarily meaningful just because it's pressing, and vice versa. Certain things are both, like big projects with close deadlines, but most things are either one or the other. For example, networking is important but not urgent, something to schedule later. A meeting where you're not a key player might be urgent but not important, something to put less effort into or even delegate. Lots of things are neither. Applying this matrix to my own personal life has brought me an unwitting dose of clarity. I might categorize reading the news as important but not always critically urgent. How might our news comprehension actually improve if we paused our consumption until tomorrow, or even reserved it all for the end of the week? For me, looking at the stars or holding Casey's hand might not be timely matters, but they are meaningful. A bout of social media drama might feel urgent, but it's almost never important. On second thought, it's not even urgent. It's "something that should not be done at all." The more I ponder it, the vast majority of hourly "problems" I encounter are neither urgent nor important enough to require my entire, immediate attention, much less full-throttle panic. Signs point to time being more plentiful than it seems.

I am enraptured by humans' perception of time, particularly by how accurately our bodies can track its passage with circadian rhythms (our cells' internal clocks, which are near-perfectly timed to earth's twenty-four-hour light-dark cycle), but in contrast, how our minds are so good at warping it. So many of my favorite thinkers have been plagued by time's wondrous pliancy. In her 1928 novel, *Orlando*, Virginia Woolf remarked, "An hour, once it lodges in the queer element of the human spirit, may be stretched to fifty or a hundred times its clock length; on the other hand, an hour may be accurately represented on the timepiece of the mind by one second. This extraordinary discrepancy between time on the clock and time in the mind is less known than it should be and deserves fuller investigation." In 1955, Albert Einstein wrote a letter to the grieving family of his late friend Michele Besso that said, "People like us who believe in physics know that the distinction between past, present, and future is only a stubbornly persistent illusion."

How striking it has always been that the same six hours can slip by like pebbles in a rainstick if you're tipsy at a concert, swaying to a band you love, but will drag on agonizingly if you're at the DMV, or stoned at a party with too many crooked-faced strangers.

When Casey and I fell in love, those first few months sped by like a magnetic levitation train. A decade after we'd last seen each other in Baltimore, we discovered that we had actually lived two blocks from each other in L.A. for years and never knew it. A jocular DM exchange led us to a shuffleboard dive bar down the street for $2 Blue Moons on nostalgia's tab. To me, Casey looked the same as he did at fifteen, clean-shaven and boyish, but with the addition of tortoiseshell spectacles that suggested pedigree. He'd graduated from an Ivy League school—I thought he'd surely gone all Brooks Brothers by now. Meanwhile, I was a beauty editor with too many highlights; he was nervous I'd bleached my spirit, too. But there's no intoxicant stronger than the mix of familiarity and surprise. It took us about five minutes after reuniting for Casey and me to decide we wanted to be together. Or *was* it only five minutes? Time extended and contracted like an exercise band. One morning early in our courtship, I accidentally waltzed into my workplace three hours late, because we'd spent all that time in the front seat of my car just counting the specks in each other's irises. Everything felt so uncharted and euphoric then, a self-made cocktail of eustress, that staring at each other's faces constituted half a day's activity. Those months of new romance whirred by, but through the hazy lens of recollection, they seem to have lasted a Jupiter year.*

How much newness we experience largely defines our sense of time. Without memory, time doesn't exist, and the borders bookending clockable events are the checkpoints we need to chart its passage. That's why time felt so twisted during COVID-19 lockdown. A 2020 survey conducted in the U.K. revealed that more than 80 percent of participants felt like quarantime was distorted. We didn't have as many experiences worth recording then—simple life things, like knocking back your first oyster at the new bistro in town or chancing upon an incredible wool coat in the haystack of a thrift store, or even bad kinds of newness, like awkward first dates and crusty road trip motels. The pandemic swept our brains out to sea, so while time felt grievously sluggish in the moment, when we look back, we wonder where it all went. When you fall in love, the opposite takes place. All that novelty between me and Casey caused us to be thoroughly present, elongating the hours to a hundred times their clock length. This is also why childhood feels so long—because everything was brand-new. Or at least brand-new to you.

The recency illusion.

It is really no wonder that this cognitive bias took such hold of us during an age when people found themselves in a state of sharp, fitful worry but also universally starved of the natural borders necessary to keep time. It is no accident

---

* It takes almost twelve full earth years for Jupiter to revolve around the sun once.

we all clung so fervently to *60 Minutes*'s alien story, even killjoys like me who didn't really believe. The UAP were a threat, an opportunity, and a fantasy all at the same time.

The news is important, but we are not built for it, these robber barons thieving our attention. Thinking about clocks and queer human spirits, I have to suspect if headlines and social media feeds can so easily speed time up, perhaps we can consciously coach the mind to slow it back down. What if we could regain a crumb of control over our temporal perception, at least for long enough to remember that whenever we encounter a digital smoke signal, we are only guesstimating its salience?

So far, my favorite strategy has to do with awe. Different from joy, awe is the kind of humbling wonder associated with immersion in nature, live music, collective dance, spiritual rituals, and psychedelics. It's the particular emotion that arises "when we encounter vast mysteries we don't understand," wrote Dacher Keltner, UC Berkeley psychology professor and author of *Awe: The New Science of Everyday Wonder and How It Can Transform Your Life*. Even in small doses, awe moves people to feel less impatient, less self-focused, more generous, and eager to spend money on experiences over possessions.[*] In *The Creative Act: A Way of Being*, record producer Rick Rubin endorses awe as an artistic tool: "As artists, we seek

---

[*] Simply looking at nature motivates us to be less materialistic. In one study published by *Psychological Science*, participants who'd just taken in a wondrous outdoor view were more likely than the control group to report that they'd rather spend $50 on a Broadway show ticket than a nice wristwatch.

to restore our childlike perception. . . . Most of what we see in the world holds the potential to inspire astonishment if looked at from a less jaded perspective."

Awe is not unlike the Greek understanding of ecstasy, meaning "to stand to the side of reality," or the flow states described by psychologist Mihaly Csikszentmihalyi. A person is "in flow" when their attention is so effortlessly consumed by an enjoyable challenge that "time disappears, you forget yourself, you feel part of something larger." Csikszentmihalyi argued that putting more of everyday life in that "flow channel" is a key to well-being. The craft of time dilation and contraction is also a benefit of mindfulness. A 2014 *Frontiers in Psychology* paper determined that when expert mindfulness meditators hyperfocus on sensory moments, they experience "a slowing down of time and an expansion of the experienced present." These results don't require a lifetime of training; in 2023, a study published in *JAMA Psychiatry* reported that people who received just eight weeks of mindfulness lessons enjoyed a decrease in stress comparable to the effects of Lexapro.

The entire summer of 2021, that damned alien season, I woke up almost every morning with nauseating anxiety, my heart a trapped hummingbird. There was no uniquely "good" reason for my trouble, but rather a bevy of nonunique ones: the pandemic, the political climate, a burst of professional distress, the slow death of a beloved pet. The things people go through. After shooting awake in cold sweats for enough consecutive months, it grew difficult to imagine how the feeling might ever end. That is, until I sent myself on a solo excursion to the Blue Ridge Mountains of western North Carolina. I felt almost silly with relief when all it took to emotionally recalibrate (for a few weeks, at least) was spending four days amid those billion-year-old cobalt peaks. A 2017 study from the *Journal of Environmental Psychology* reported that, compared to city strolls, taking walks in nature elevated mood, decreased stress, and relaxed participants' sense of time. I can corroborate: During my stretches in the woods, I felt "in flow." Half a week in Appalachia rendered me a sprig of sea kelp floating along at exactly the right pace, a pace determined by a force greater than the news cycle and certainly greater than me. As *New York Times* columnist Nicholas Kristof wrote in 2012, "Perhaps wilderness is an antidote to our postindustrial self-absorption."

Gazing up at a deciduous oak isn't some enchanted solution to everyone's problems, of course. But, where the recency illusion is concerned, connecting with the physical world we were made for opens up a tiny mental wormhole, allowing us to recast time for just long enough to remember that a headline in your feed is not a predator in the bushes or crop circle in your backyard. With that spare glint of awareness, we can determine with better clarity if a piece of news is more deserving of our precious time and cognitive resources than the one we were worried about yesterday. I'm convinced we have more power to select what's worthy of our attention than we think. Hyper-advanced aerial technology is impressive, and so are news algorithms, but I am far more in awe of the mind.

Maybe we've been the futuristic aliens all along.

✸

SEVEN

THE SCAMMER WITHIN
A note on overconfidence bias

It was just the kind of juicy, low-stakes true-crime story I live for. On January 6, 1995, under a glimmering canopy of midday sun, a forty-four-year-old white man named McArthur Wheeler waltzed into a couple of Pittsburgh banks and held up the tellers at gunpoint. Wheeler was impossible to miss. No ski mask, no shame—in the security camera screengrabs, the fellow looks downright cozy in a navy zip-up sweatshirt and knockoff Oakley sunglasses, which repose coolly atop his salt-and-pepper combover. A local news channel obtained and broadcast the footage, after which Wheeler promptly found himself in police custody . . . and totally aghast. "But I wore the juice," he protested. Wheeler meant lemon juice. His getaway partner heard the stuff could be used as invisible ink, and they both figured if Wheeler smeared it all over his face, his features would look obscured to cameras. Wheeler wasn't on drugs; he was determined mentally stable. He was just, well, overconfident.

Beginning to examine the literature on excess confidence, I came across Wheeler's case right away. Self-satirizing crime stories like his are irresistible to me. Though if we're picking and choosing genres, my taste in true crime is really the subcategory labeled "true con." Rather than tales of everyday people getting murdered, I prefer hearing about wealthy people getting financially screwed: art theft, wine fraud, schemes both Ponzi and pyramid. I don't know why murder never really did it for me. I have this theory that white ladies tend to rubberneck at serial killers the same way white men are obsessed with World War II. As easily as all those *Saving Private Ryan* fanatics can picture getting drafted, murder "junkies" can fold their freshly laundered undies to a soundtrack of gruesome whodunit podcasts, imagining themselves shackled in the basement of a Swedish cannibal or dismembered in a lake, next to the severed limbs of the fair suburbanite in the story. Ogling these subjects seems like a twisted empathy exercise for populations who don't typically face enough material violence in their daily lives to spoil the entertainment. It's also another illusion of control. Like a macabre rehearsal, the more murder and war documentaries we consume, the more secure we hope to feel in our hypothetical ability to survive such horrors if we had to.

But I should mind my own business. That high-end con artists have always been more my cup of tea deserves its own critique. I have to wonder if my transfixion with grifters like Elizabeth Holmes, the billionaire health tech CEO turned convicted fraudster, or Simon Leviev, the dating app Ponzi schemer known as "the Tinder Swindler," might stem from the fact that I'm terrified I might actually *admire* them. After all, overconfidence like theirs is a trait America characteristically celebrates. "Fake it till you make it" is considered a wise proverb in this culture. I did a lot of community theater as a child and heard this sentiment from our local playhouses' bescarved directors all the time: "If a casting agent asks if you can skateboard, or tap-dance, or ride a kangaroo, even if you can't, just say yes!" Early in life, I learned that overpromising your capabilities and simply crossing your fingers it'll all work out was a praiseworthy talent. How troubling, though, is the fact that Elizabeth Holmes learned her overconfidence not from criminal trickster Charles Ponzi but from celebrated genius Steve Jobs. When the Apple CEO presented his very first iPhone model, it didn't work as described, and there was no guarantee it ever would. When does confidence go from aspirational to tacky to worthy of prosecution?

At one time, I might've guessed expertise had something to do with it, but I'd have been wrong. A year after McArthur Wheeler's botched bank robberies, his guffaw-worthy incompetence was immortalized in the 1996 *World Almanac*. That's where Cornell psychologist David Dunning thumbed across it and was inspired to examine the empirical relationship between ignorance and confidence. In a now much quoted study, the professor and his graduate student conceived the *Dunning-Kruger effect*, a pattern where people with the littlest knowledge on a subject consistently prove themselves likeliest to overvalue their expertise. Since its publication, whenever swaths of nonexperts publicly claim jurisdiction on subjects from parenting to politics, commentators have called upon the Dunning-Kruger effect to explain away their foolishness. It's such a satisfying way to dismiss your adversaries: The smarter they *think* they are, the denser they must be. And if you're wise enough to reference the Dunning-Kruger effect, then it obviously can't apply to you.

It turns out, though, that the Dunning-Kruger effect didn't say quite what many of us thought it did. Upon closer examination, the famous experiment did not account for enough social and psychological factors (mood, age, etc.) to prove definitively that knowing very little is what causes a person to think they know a lot. Most people, even experts, systematically overestimate their skills. "It's just that experts do that over a narrower range," clarified Dunning in an interview with McGill University twenty years after his original paper. "The lesson of the effect was always about how we should be humble and cautious about ourselves." Not another excuse to feel supercilious.

In reality, one powerful and volatile intuition is responsible for criminals as laughable as Wheeler, as obnoxious as the Tinder Swindler, and as sophisticated as Holmes. It's the same quality that yields sweeping worship of business "disruptors" like Steve Jobs, but in the wrong quantities, it also positions them for rapid falls from grace. Silicon Valley CEOs and felons (tomato, to-mah-to) are not the only figures who bow to this cognitive kink. It also shows up in subtler, more pedestrian behaviors and judgments that most people make every day. The inclination appears in three key forms: people overvalue their actual skills, express excessive certainty in their evaluations, and overcredit themselves with positive outcomes. Austerely, this trifecta is labeled *overconfidence bias*.

Confronted with the idea of too much confidence, it's hard not to think, *this is a bias* other *people enjoy, not me*, especially among those of us who find ourselves tormented by self-critique. Reporting on overconfidence has been an exercise in self-reflection; when all I want to do is wag my finger at a few choice egomaniacs I've encountered in my life (god, you have no idea how badly I want to name names), I come across another study that forces me to look inward instead. Since its coining in the 1960s, overconfidence bias has been documented all over our fair planet across a bevy of experiments. Researchers have deduced that unless a person is navigating some major psychological interference like PTSD or clinical depression,*

---

* With cosmic irony, research on superiority complexes has found that people with depression assess their talents more objectively than others, a symptom termed "depressive realism." A 2013 paper published in the *Proceedings of the National Academy of Sciences* noted that people with weak connectivity between their brain's frontal lobe (responsible for our sense of self) and striatum (part of the reward system) overall thought more highly of themselves than those with stronger

nearly everyone alive naturally overestimates their moral compass, everyday skills, and common knowledge with a consistency I still find hard to accept. Well over half of folks surveyed think themselves above average at driving,* cooking, and sex, even though only 50 percent can be. Given general knowledge tests (questions like, "What country has the highest life expectancy?" and "Who was the Ancient Greek god of the sun?"), most participants predict their answers to be 10 percent to 25 percent more accurate than they really are. "[Overconfidence] is the whole foundation of 'Pinterest Fails,'" commented Rachel Torres, a licensed school psychologist and PhD candidate at Chapman University, referencing online craft tutorials gone cockeyed. "You see someone bake a batch of cat-shaped cupcakes and you think, oh, I can make that. It's going to be beautiful. Then it turns out looking like barf." Indeed, I can safely say that I've never prepared a baked good that didn't look like bile, and yet I'm not at all ready to label myself a poorer than average baker. The data is plain as day, and still, my overconfidence persists. What, oh what, is the meaning of this horrendous ego curse?

---

connections between the two areas. Dopamine neurotransmitters located in the striatum inhibit connectivity to the frontal lobe, like rocks in a dam, so the more dopamine you have, the less connectivity between the two regions, and the more blissfully flattering your self-perception will be. Conversely, depleted dopamine = more depression = more realistic self-evaluation. But the former is what's described as "normal." Worshiping at our own altars without question is considered the "mentally healthy" state.

* A famous 1981 study by Swedish decision scientist Ola Svenson found that a whole 93 percent of respondents fancy themselves better behind the wheel than most.

As unbecoming as bigheadedness may be, it historically had its merits. A 2011 *Nature* study proposed that natural selection may have favored a swollen ego, as it enhanced resolve and perseverence, made it easier to bluff opponents in conflict, and generated a self-fulfilling prophecy where self-assuredness alone fostered better chances of survival. Political science researchers from Britain, Germany, and Switzerland tested the survival benefits of overconfidence by conducting a series of experimental war games. Participants were asked to assess the weakness of neighboring countries, represented as squares on a grid, and then decide whether or not to attack. The study concluded that while overconfident participants were more likely than anyone else to blitz opponents unprovoked and overall fought more battles, when it came to the end of the war, the victor was always someone who'd behaved overconfidently. The researchers analyzed that even though overconfident parties were expected to lose more wars, they also entered more wars, "effectively 'buying more lottery tickets' in the competition for survival." Sure, some overconfident states reached too far and got clobbered, but by chance, others enjoyed back-to-back wins, receiving positive feedback each time that they really were as great as they thought and should continue with their conquests. So they expanded quickly, growing more powerful from the resources they progressively gained. When you keep winning, what incentive is there to reevaluate? As journalist Roger Lowenstein wrote in his book *When Genius Failed*, "There is nothing like success to blind one to the possibility of failure."

In civilized society, overconfidence still comes with advantages: attracting friends and followers, boosting morale. The bias can be a career asset. In both professional and semi-professional settings—from Wall Street to the PTA—the most adored and respected figures are tragically not always the most competent, but rather the most self-possessed. "Whether [people] are good or not is kind of irrelevant," argued UC Berkeley psychologist Cameron Anderson, who studies overconfidence, politics, and business leadership. Notably, *feigned* confidence will not do. Anderson noted that genuine self-assurance can be measured by certain verbal and physical cues, like speaking both early and often in a low, relaxed tone. Onlookers are sensitive to these indicators and don't appreciate bullshit, but only when the bullshitter himself does not buy it. A 2014 study in *Scientific Reports* concluded that overconfidence is promoted by the very act of "self-deceptive bluffing," the kind of deep con where you don't simply act like you're better than you are, you honestly believe it. So you have this feedback loop of overpromising and overconfidence, and as long as a person's bluffing doesn't stretch all the way to "lemon juice will make me invisible," these warped self-assessments are stunningly effective.

They can make you famous. I've never been to war, but living in Los Angeles, I sense overconfidence like air pollution every time I leave my house. Aspiring entertainers treat this town like a battlefield. The vocabularies of war and fame are alarmingly similar: "shooting your shot," "crushing" and "killing" it. In 2022, a Bloomberg survey found that

98 percent of American middle and high schoolers expressed the desire to be internet famous.* NINETY-EIGHT PERCENT. The coalescence of Hollywood and social media explicitly encourages a culture of self-deceptive bluffing, as if users are owed commercialized clout simply because it exists to claim. Thanks to TikTok, becoming famous overnight for merely existing in front of a camera became an unprecedented and intoxicating possibility. Call me a curmudgeon, but as paths to success continue to resemble a (rigged) lottery, I'm concerned that the appeal of mastering a craft offline and sharing it with well-calibrated aplomb will fade in favor of "shooting your shot," exchanging bluffery for ticket after ticket in the viral game.

The risks of overconfidence extend far past all-you-can-consume comedy skits and skincare routines. Inconveniently, the modern mind tends to exhibit the most overconfidence precisely in scenarios where accurate judgments are hardest to make. These include new and unpredictable technology (AI, interplanetary travel), natural disasters (hurricanes, climate change), and polarizing political figures (I can think of one or two). In our maximalist age, a time of billionaires racing toward technological advancement, that fact seems more foreboding than ever. A 2018 paper published in Cambridge's *Journal of Financial and Quantitative Analysis* found that overconfident CEOs were likelier

---

* Three years earlier, a survey by the Harris Poll and Lego determined that three times as many British, Chinese, and American children wanted to be YouTubers as astronauts.

to make overly optimistic promises and downplay negative developments, bringing on massive lawsuits. Overconfidence is to blame for contemporary calamities including stock market nosedives, medical misdiagnoses, and technological failures—like 1986's *Challenger* space shuttle disaster, before which NASA estimated its fatality risk was just one in 100,000.

Overconfidence bias also shows up constantly in crime. It applies not only to the actions of criminals like McArthur Wheeler (and his savvier peers), but also to outsiders' judgments of defendants. In the late 1980s, a comprehensive review of wrongful convictions in the U.S. uncovered 350 instances where innocent defendants were found guilty of capital crimes "beyond a reasonable doubt." In five of those cases, the error was discovered before sentencing. The other 345 were not so lucky: 67 were sentenced to prison for up to twenty-five years, 139 were sentenced to life in prison, and another 139 were sentenced to death. At the time of the review, 23 defendants had already been executed. As Wesleyan University psychologist Scott Plous summed up in his book *The Psychology of Judgment and Decision Making*, out of all our cognitive biases, perhaps none is "more prevalent and more potentially catastrophic" than overconfidence.

Last winter, while devouring a Bernie Madoff documentary, I was struck like a handcuff to the wrist with the notion that maybe scammer stories enthrall me so much because of a latent fear that I am my own con artist. Every time I step forward in my career, it's evidence that I'm running one big Ponzi scheme. Any day now, the FBI will materialize on my doorstep, my imaginary sons having turned me in with a stack of forged documents. Perhaps overconfidence is so fascinating to me because I simultaneously crave it and am terrified I already have too much of it. American culture provides such mixed messaging on the matter of confidence. Flaunt your accomplishments, but don't be a narcissist. Be authentic, but also be perfect. Tell the casting director you can tap-dance even if you can't and someone else is better for the job. I wish I knew how much confidence was the "right" amount to have. How much will help you succeed professionally and feel internally content but not cross over into such delirium that you risk causing damage and annoying the living daylights out of everyone?

Chapman psychologist Rachel Torres studies imposter syndrome, which is sometimes framed as the opposite of the Dunning-Kruger effect. Torres and I have been friends since college; we met in a creative writing workshop, and I always admired her scholarly commitment, even as a cocky college student, to ensuring that her opinions were elegantly supported before opening her mouth. It only makes sense that she'd go on to study this "syndrome," which she defines as the persistent self-perception that one is phony or incompetent, even as they're swimming in evidence to the contrary. "I experience imposter syndrome a lot in my work, despite having years of training and all these credentials. I show up to meetings feeling like a fraud," confessed Torres, who is not only decorated with several master's degrees but has won every award and scholarship I've ever seen her pursue. Imposter syndrome shows up not unlike a workplace-specific anxiety disorder, said Torres. Symptoms include cycles of negative thinking, self-mistrust, and minimizing accomplishments. (Sounds like a typical day at the office to me.) "Do you personally know anyone who does not experience imposter syndrome?" I asked her. Torres took a beat, a sigh, then responded plainly, "No."

Torres shares my obsession with the true-con genre. We gabbed extensively about the Elizabeth Holmes case as news unfolded that her billion-dollar health tech company Theranos was a sham. I've long wondered if Holmes experienced glints of imposter syndrome like everyone else and just barreled too far past them, because she was a WASPy American with a dream to be the next Steve Jobs, and "fake it till you make it," right? First described in the 1970s, imposter syndrome was born of a moment in the American workforce when the civil rights movement, second-wave feminism, and a booming post–World War II economy ushered marginalized workers into a labor market that was constructed for white men's success. "Crimes aside, our society is not set up for Elizabeth Holmes to repeat and pull off Steve Jobs's story the same way our society is not set up for a female CEO at all," said Torres. The media massacred Holmes for her bizarre behavior, deep voice, and "creepy" eye contact. "But would our response have been different if she were a man? Yes," Torres continued. "Would she have gotten farther or gone in a different direction? Maybe. Would her entire story have been different if she were a queer person of color? Probably."*

Torres speculated that nearly everyone alive experiences some degree of imposter syndrome, even highly privileged figures with charisma to burn, even certain types of narcissists who appear publicly untouchable but are privately plagued by self-alienation and loathing. Aside from proven sociopaths, the condition spares no one, not even society's most prized citizens. As such, imposter syndrome might not even really "exist." Mounting research indicates it is not a natural phenomenon. "Many attribute imposter syndrome fully to societal and systemic causes," Torres explained. It's a disease of the system, and a recent one at that: Only in the 1980s, with rises in entrepreneurship and the dawn of career counseling, did professional success and "life purpose" become indivisible. Combine this conflation with the deeply embedded meritocracy myth, and of course a majority of the population would feel like if we're not professionally thriving, then we must be worthless, and if we *are* thriving, then we must be frauds.

"The 40-hour work week was built to allow white men to succeed at work while their wives would care for all of the family's child and home responsibilities," noted Shahamat Uddin, a journalist who covers the intersection of Desi

---

* Not to mention, Holmes didn't go to jail for making overconfident promises to everyday people, but rather for making overconfident promises to wealthy investors.

identity and queerness, in an op-ed on workplace racism. "I come to every interview, job shift, meeting, 20 minutes early because I know that I have to fight the expectation of Brown tardiness . . . I know that I need to work twice as hard to prove that I belong there." The willfully "diseased" American labor market was not built for women and people of color to exist at all, much less feel foundationally accepted.

Torres and I agreed there's something eerie about figures like the Tinder Swindler and Bernie Madoff, whose actions demonstrate no sign of imposter syndrome. "I mean, at what point," Torres lamented, "did they come to believe that sunshine shoots out of their ass?"

Overconfidence isn't just a style of behavior, though—it's also a mental posture. On one hand, the bias motivates commanders to go to war and lucky devils to over-credit themselves for their success; but, in a quieter context, it's also what affords people the entitlement to loaf about the sofa, thumb through the internet or watch reality television, and click their teeth in judgment at others' imbecilic gaffes. If one were to ask me if I think I am above or below average in terms of common human decency, my instinct would of course be to say the former. This kind of self-inflation is innate. When we do something that yields a poor outcome, our automatic reaction is usually one of surprise. Accused of moral wrongdoing, the average person is quick to turn defensive, in large part because it's an earnest shock to believe that *we*, with our tender hearts and fair intentions, could've screwed up.

Women can actually be more morally punishing than men. A 2018 study published in the *Personality and Social Psychology Bulletin* found that for much of history, women were viewed as less moral, due to their higher "perceived emotionality." Having feelings was rumored to impede moral reasoning. However, according to the study, while significant evidence suggests that women are in fact *not* more emotional than men overall, they do tend to display higher "self-conscious moral emotions and empathic concern." These qualities caused study participants to report lower intentions to commit "morally questionable actions" that could result in personal or professional benefits but cause harm along the way, like bending rules and lying during negotiations. Most of the women surveyed also considered these acts "less permissible" and worthy of "harsher moral condemnation" than male participants.

Empathic concern is good, it's everything really, but I can't say I love the moral reproach piece. It seems to align with the self-serving dimension of overconfidence bias: the tendency to attribute positive outcomes to ourselves while blaming others for negative results. I noticed self-serving bias mushroom-cloud throughout the many social reckonings of the late 2010s and early 2020s, including protests for antiracism and abortion rights, particularly among women sitting in privileged seats, who expressed concern for others' pain but didn't want to be held responsible for it themselves.

I asked Koa Beck, journalist and author of *White Feminism: From the Suffragettes to Influencers and Who They*

Leave Behind, if self-serving attitudes impact modern social justice movements. She answered, "I notice especially on Twitter and Instagram, there is a very hot crucible of white women calling out other white women, and that seems to carry some sort of currency in these social spheres. There are incentives now when you critique somebody's racial illiteracy, transphobia, or classism. Online platforms have underscored and quantified ways to build your own platform based on finger-pointing."

Semiconsciously, said Beck, some social media users not only highlight but capitalize on others' missteps, specifically ones that remind them of those they'd nearly made themselves, as a way to "get in front" of the narrative. Say a white, able-bodied user comments a zingy critique on a stranger's social media post for their insensitive use of the word "crazy" and receives two hundred likes for doing so. That might look like activism to some, but self-serving bias is also at play. The offender's mistake reminds the complainant of how virtuous they are for having avoided the same foible, however narrowly. Calling them out becomes too tempting to resist, especially when the dopamine bath of all those approving likes awaits. A favorite quote from the book *Mistakes Were Made (But Not by Me)* by psychologists Carol Tavris and Elliot Aronson reads, "It's the people who *almost* decide to live in glass houses who throw the first stones."

You know what's ironic? The expertise of *other people* is actually what allows us to think we know more than we do. The 2017 book *The Knowledge Illusion* by Philip Fernbach and Steven Sloman opened with a Yale study in which graduate students were invited to rate how well they understood ordinary gadgets, like toilets and zippers. Then, they were asked to write thorough, bit-by-bit breakdowns of how these apparatuses worked and rate their understanding once more. The task seemed to show the students their own deficiencies—their second self-assessments plummeted. Even zippers, as it happens, are more sophisticated than we realize. *Someone* knows how zippers work, of course. Someone invented the zipper so we could all use it easily enough to take for granted. That kind of specialization and collaboration is something at which our species is uniquely skilled. So smooth is our cooperation that we can scarcely discern where another person's comprehension starts and ours ends. According to *The Knowledge Illusion*, we divide our cognitive labor so naturally that we're left with "no sharp boundary between one person's ideas and knowledge" and "those of other [group] members."

We can't even identify where search engines' knowledge starts and ours drops off. Via web search, one can access answers to any question in less than a second. How far away is the moon? What is overconfidence bias? But this instantaneous ability doesn't mean the wisdom instantaneously becomes ours. Studies show that not only do we swiftly forget the information we learn via web search, we actually forget that we forgot it—we confuse the internet's knowledge for our own. Some refer to this mental hiccup as "the

Google effect." AI language tools like ChatGPT* make the boundaries separating our individual knowledge pools even more porous.

From human to human, at least, our fuzzy brain boundaries have an upside: They lend themselves to innovation. Every time someone makes a meaningful discovery, they unlock a new level of nescience. Gaps in understanding drive us forward. If I had to know exactly what I wanted to say in this book before putting pen to paper, I would never have started nor finished. If master's degrees in gender studies were required to engage in grassroots advocacy, we would have no feminist movements at all. In 1977, writing about the intersection of activism and creativity, Audre Lorde said, "Sometimes we drug ourselves with dreams of new ideas. The head will save us. The brain alone will set us free." There are no new ideas, wrote Lorde, just new ways of making them felt: "We must constantly encourage ourselves and each other to attempt the heretical actions our dreams imply." Sometimes, overconfident delusions give us the nerve to keep gunning for a better world.

I don't know where in life I learned that humility was synonymous with self-deprecation (community theater again?),

---

* Speaking of ego, in early 2023 a friend asked if I'd ever prompted ChatGPT to write something "in the style of Amanda Montell." I hadn't, but after the seed was planted, my navel-gazing curiosity got the best of me. I asked the chatbot to write a paragraph defining cognitive biases in my voice. ("You're so weird. It's a Saturday. Get off the internet and go outside," Casey told me the moment he learned I'd done this.) Reader, the exercise was bizarre. The bot's closing line went, "Your mind is a playground, my love, and biases are the cheeky little bullies on the monkey bars." I was simultaneously amused and offended. Do I really sound like that???

but it's a misconception I harbored for years. Not until I came across an entry in the American Psychological Association's dictionary did I realize humility is defined by "a low focus on the self, an accurate (not over- or underestimated) sense of one's accomplishments and worth, and an acknowledgment of one's limitations, imperfections, mistakes, gaps in knowledge, and so on." Every hour I've wasted worrying that other people were keeping track of my failures, nitpicking my malapropisms and fashion faux pas, was not humility, it was just more self-focus. Social incentives to broadcast career milestones and glitzy engagements—but not before a dramatic recounting of all the "no's" you received before you ever got a "yes"—pervert genuine humility into just another stunt in the ego Olympics. "Whether it looks like extreme insecurity or overconfidence, too much self-focus on either end of the spectrum is not good," said Torres. "It prevents what I think many of us are ultimately trying to do, which is simply to be present, connect, and show up for life."

In a culture that not only tolerates but actively endorses self-deceptive bluffing, how can we rebrand confidence as something that *requires* the ability to reevaluate, or even retreat, rather than attack? No one can evade screwing up entirely, but we *are* capable of noticing when something is no longer reasonable or workable. We can stop and change course. No one wants to end up on the evening news with lemon juice on their face.

Encouragingly, a 2021 study published in the *Philosophical Transactions of the Royal Society* found that when confidence is well aligned with performance, and metacognitive ability* is high, then subjects "tend to be less confident after making errors, and, therefore, also open to corrective information." In my own life, I've decided to start rewarding people more than I ordinarily would when they admit their mistakes, or else they just won't. We cannot perceive self-doubt as a weakness, and we shouldn't demand undying certainty even from experts, or they will surely bullshit us in order to meet that expectation. WASPs in turtlenecks will overpromise eager investors. They'll press launch before the rocket is ready.

In 2011, those war game experiments found that top-performing states actually had a lukewarm level of overconfidence. The winners were never grossly overconfident nor were they totally humble, suggesting that where confidence is concerned, there is an "optimal margin of illusion." The study concluded, "Individuals with a more nuanced approach—even a biased one—do better than the extremes."

But I think what I really want is to treat life less like a war. Wouldn't we have less imposter syndrome and fewer actual imposters if we just lowered our standards a bit? Modern productivity dogma encourages us to act fast and milk our exceptionalism for all it's worth. Under that kind of pressure, perhaps the truest rebellion is to embrace our ordinariness. In everyday life, if we could not only tolerate the discomfort but wholeheartedly embrace our own lack of expertise,

---

* awareness of one's own thought processes

then we might have a far better chance of showing others the same grace. Then perhaps life might feel, at the very least, less agitating. At most, we might even find peace.

How's this: Let's stoop below average at 50 percent of all we do. We'll relish it. The commonness. Next time we have a question, let's hold out for as long as we humanly can before googling the answer. It'll be erotic. Like edging before a climax. It's quite nice, I am learning, just to wonder indefinitely. To never have certain answers. To sit down, be humble, and not even dare to know.

EIGHT

HATERS ARE MY MOTIVATORS
A note on the illusory truth effect

My relationship to truth changed forever because of a lie about wedding flowers.

I was looking into the sinister history of marriage traditions for an episode of the cult-themed podcast I'd been hosting for a year and change. The "cult" of weddings was that week's subject of critique. I'd always harbored an intuitive contempt for the bridal industry's conformist liturgy and consumerism—the idea that blood diamonds, matching bridesmaids' frocks, demands of your loved one's unbridled obedience, and $20,000 in debt were all just part of the "fun." I knew I wasn't alone in that feeling, I just needed some lurid evidentiary backup. Perusing sources from *Brides* magazine to Reddit, I kept finding the same yarn spun again and again about the origins of the bridal bouquet. The much repeated claim stated that because medieval peasants bathed so infrequently, only about once a year, brides learned to carry bunches of fragrant herbs down the aisle to mask their tangy stenches. The modern-day popularity of the June wedding, these articles stated, derives from the old-time tradition of enjoying your annual wash in late spring.

I *cherish* a fun fact. Chancing upon a gold bullion of dinner table fodder makes me come alive; so, while these reports of filthy feudal fiancées gave off their own odor, one of "too good to be true" urban legend, they were repeated so consistently and offered such juicy entertainment value, I thought, what reason do I have not to pass them along? I performed a subconscious calculation, weighing the likelihood of these stories' veracity against the impact either way, and in the end, I decided yes, I shall repeat them on air. In my recounting, I hedged with words like "I guess" and "I read that," but it didn't matter. The day the podcast episode aired, one listener giddily tweeted: "LMAO I just learned on a podcast that the reason brides carry bouquets is because in Medieval Europe they only bathed once a year!!!!" Thousands of reshares poured in. The factoid spread like a communicable disease.

Patently less viral went the Twitter response from Dr. Eleanor Janega, a medieval historian at the London School of Economics. Janega heard the episode and chimed in that basically every piece of popular lore from the Middle Ages is a myth, including, unfortunately, this one. Just like today, bridal bouquets in the medieval period were made of flowers, arranged according to their color symbolism, not their perfume. A thousand years ago, peasants may not have delighted in indoor plumbing or obsessive twice-daily showers, but they did plenty of grooming, often in communal bathhouses.

Wash time was such a production in medieval Europe that some royals entertained guests with it, keen to show off their lavish bathing facilities and herbal elixirs. Charlemagne was known to invite fellow nobles over to join him for a rinse. Allegedly, he'd even welcome crowds of spectators to behold dozens of wealthy men literally bathing in the lap of luxury together. I don't know about you, but I find this story about a hundred times more amusing than peasants not showering very much. Plus, it has the benefit of being true.

I was not surprised to learn from Dr. Janega that the wedding origin stories I'd read and spread were the stuff of folktales. I was mildly horrified, however, at my own eagerness to share them, despite my better brain doubting their accuracy. I proceeded to contact Janega, hoping to gain some clarity on why so much mythology surrounds the Middle Ages. I was embarrassed to have to ask exactly which years were even in question here (hadn't I learned this in high school?). The thousand-year period approximately considered medieval spans from the fall of Rome in 476 AD to Martin Luther's birth in 1483. "We invent so much about the Middle Ages partially because it's the pond between ancient and modern times," Janega explained. Close enough in history to feel familiar, but long ago and far away enough to retain mystery, medieval Europe provides the perfect backdrop for both romanticization and nightmare—fairy princesses* and

---

* Modernity has rendered us so magically overthoughtful that some have started glamorizing the "quaint" lives of Dark Ages paupers. A much-circulated 2019 headline suggested, "The average American worker takes less vacation time than a medi-

torture chambers.* It isn't terribly difficult to fact-check a historical folk tale. Why, then, even with all the accessibility and collective power of the internet, do such falsehoods prevail? And why had I, ostensibly a proud hater of mistruths, perpetuated them?

We can assign much of the blame to a bias known as the *illusory truth effect*—our penchant to trust a statement as factual simply because we've heard it multiple times. Characterized by the power of repetition to make something false "sound true," the illusory truth effect has been demonstrated using a bevy of stimuli, from fake news headlines and marketing claims to rumors, trivia, and internet memes. The bias explains why, until I was eighteen years old, I was genuinely certain that if you swallowed a piece of gum, it would take seven years to digest. But it's also how political propaganda is able to spread so effortlessly, like an X-Acto knife slicing through wrapping paper. The illusory truth effect's influence can be as benign as believing medieval brides stank worse than they did or as corrosive as the myth that people who use the welfare system are lazy. With illusory truth, entire legends and genres about individuals and societies

---

eval peasant." But where provincial PTO is concerned, Janega cleared the air: "They might've had a couple extra days off work each month for religious holidays, but if you're a peasant, and almost everyone was, the cow still has to get milked, you still need to chop firewood and stoke the fire, and if it's harvest season, it doesn't matter if you get the day off. When you think of the Middle Ages, some picture a cottagecore fantasy, but it's all well and good until you're plowing a field with no tractor."

* A staple of medieval torture museums is the iron maiden, a spikey metal cabinet, which was actually not a Dark Age device but rather a bogus invention from the late eighteenth century.

are constructed, perpetuated, and believed without reserve. At worst, masters of the bias can become tyrants. Bringing age-old storytelling traditions, like repetition and rhyme, to a political stage, public figures can mass-disseminate falsehoods on purpose, inflaming bigotry as a means of bolstering their own power. On the flip side, these language techniques infuse pleasure into learning real facts. They also encourage us to give information that's been corroborated by several sources more weight than random, one-off anecdotes. Like all biases, the sword of illusory truth is double-edged.

In 1993, Northwestern researchers Alice Eagly and Shelly Chaiken published a book titled *The Psychology of Attitudes*, in which they argued that when people lack the knowledge, literacy, or motivation to critically evaluate a message, they rely on simple heuristics, like "familiar sayings tend to be credible." It's the path of least resistance: If a nugget of information is easy to absorb, like "Smelly peasants are the reason bridal bouquets exist," it makes us *want* to believe it. Repetition is like a cognitive Tums, aiding in informational digestion. When you come across a sentiment twice and then three times, you start responding to it more quickly, your brain misinterpreting fluency as accuracy. Familiarity breeds comfort, but it also builds an immunity to unlearning and relearning, even in instances where you weren't that attached to the knowledge in the first place—like the fake origins of wedding flowers.

"To replace a previous thought with new information would mean admitting that what you thought before was wrong," said Dr. Moiya McTier, a science communicator and author of *The Milky Way: An Autobiography of Our Galaxy*. According to McTier, dismissing a claim gets trickier every time you encounter it in the wild. Swiftly, we build up a resistance to facts that contradict what we've grown cozily accustomed to. "I am genuinely afraid of this," confessed McTier, who told me she suffers a recurring nightmare (one that I sadly lived) about publicly spreading something she heard a few times but that turned out to be hogwash. The trouble is that we don't sort the things we learn at confidence intervals. Instead, we treat everything filed away in our minds as equally true. As McTier put it, "My brain doesn't separate 'things that I'm very sure about' and 'things that I'm less sure about.' It just stores all my knowledge as knowledge." Even for trained scientists, when it comes to the day-to-day handling of information, processing fluency (whether or not something "rings a bell") is our default strategy for evaluating truth. Only when that fails do we turn to actual thinking.

We internalize the illusory relationship between repetition and accuracy early in life. Children as young as five are already associating the familiarity of a statement with reliability, and the habit doesn't wane in adulthood. Vanderbilt University memory scientist Lisa Fazio published a study in the *Journal of Experimental Psychology*, which found that college students fell prey to the illusory truth effect, even when a careful knowledge test later revealed they knew the correct answer. The bias is so potent, it persists even when listeners are specifically warned to look out for it. Fazio's study concluded that the effect occurred after listeners were explicitly told the source of a statement was dubious, when it was presented with qualifying language, when it was outright implausible ("Fish can breathe air"), and when it obviously violated prior knowledge ("Mercury is the largest planet in the solar system"). The illusory truth effect bested listeners regardless of whether the time between repetitions was minutes, weeks, or months. At the risk of sounding dramatic, repetition very well might be the closest thing we have to a magical spell.

In 2018, Yale psychologist Gord Pennycook ran a survey on illusory truth using fake-news headlines from the 2016 U.S. presidential campaign. He found that if participants across the political spectrum had seen a false, seemingly absurd headline just once before, it made them up to twice as likely to believe it. Headlines from the study included, "Mike Pence's Marriage Was Saved by Gay Conversion Therapy," "FBI Agent Suspected in Hillary Email Leaks Found Dead in Apparent Murder-Suicide," and "Trump to Ban All TV Shows that Promote Gay Activity Starting with *Empire* as President." Take the gay TV headline: Pennycook noted that only about 5 percent of participants who had *not* seen the claim in a prior phase of the experiment thought it was true. But of the participants who *had* seen the headline previously, 10 percent assessed it as a fact, a perception that held up when they were tested a week later. A 5 percent increase might sound fairly low, but consider that Facebook and Google, the world's two biggest news distribution platforms, have featured questionable and even full-blown conspiratorial headlines in their trending news sections. When "participants" are in the millions, and the "study" is real life, it's no wonder America's sense of truth has crumbled like medieval ruins.

Before the advent of writing systems and the mass distribution of books, the only way to learn anything without experiencing it firsthand was through oral repetition. Memorable chants, songs, poems, legends, allegories, jokes. The average human might not have been beset by information overload, but being underinformed wasn't ideal, either. For most of history, a community's elites (priests, royals, eventually the privileged scribes who were taught to read and write) guarded knowledge like precious ore. The clandestine nature of information gave these gatekeepers immense power, more than any individual holds today.

Technology later democratized information, and the folkloric traditions people had been using to spread wisdom for millennia took on new forms. Pithy Instagram quotes were the new proverbs; exaggerated headlines became our antique legends. I spoke with Butler University folklorist Dr. Tom Mould, who explained that a legend is defined by three core qualities: It's told as true but clearly carries undertones of doubt; its content is extremely difficult or impossible to confirm; and, not unlike a superstition, it helps us capture and cope with culture-wide fears. Legends don't typically survive passage when they're immediately disprovable—say, the claim that a certain harmless berry is actually deadly poisonous. Eat the berry, and you'll know right away whether or not it'll kill you. But the lore that breaking a mirror yields a curse of bad sex is tougher to evaluate. To confirm if it takes seven years to digest gum would require scalpels and scientists. And good luck verifying whether Trump had intentions to ban any TV show that "promoted gay activity." Sure, we could google our way to most answers—experts like Eleanor Janega are easier than ever to access—but the illusory truth effect is so alluring, it often deters us from doing so. Instead, we pass on the legends. We retweet. We tell the world a story we know in our heart of hearts can't be true.

Search engines may have made fact-finding easier, but language determines a fact's shareability. Using our species' favorite storytelling devices to make information more palatable can either be an educational gift or a sociopolitical weapon. Take proverbs: Historically, proverbs have offered snappy, "common sense" answers to life's more cerebral mysteries, and for the ones that most people know, there's usually a corollary that presents a counter-perspective. For instance, "The early bird gets the worm" and "Strike while the iron is hot" are inverses to "Better late than never" and "Good things come to those who wait." "Actions speak louder than words" contrasts "The pen is mightier than the sword." I grew up hearing both "Teamwork makes the dream work" and "Haters are my motivators."* These inconsistencies are

---

* A few more contradicting aphorisms: "Out of sight, out of mind" vs. "Absence makes the heart grow fonder"; "Birds of a feather flock together" vs. "Opposites attract"; the Golden Rule vs. "Nice guys finish last"; and "Haste makes waste" vs. "He who hesitates is lost."

important, because they suggest there are multiple worthy approaches to life. Things only start to get sinister when public authority figures including politicians, religious leaders, and CEOs (but also sometimes memers and podcasters) use the recipe of a proverb to market a one-sided ideology that makes no room for antidotes.

Dr. Sheila Bock, a folklorist at the University of Nevada, Las Vegas, told me that society's most repeated proverbs "are not necessarily the ones that are true, but are the ones that make 'good cultural sense.'" Tropes give speakers a framework to understand the world, and in times of stress, those tropes get more rigid. Consider America's "welfare queen" trope: In 2020, Tom Mould conducted a survey that examined the online social lore surrounding perceived "moochers" of government assistance. Mould asked his study participants to look at their social media feeds and note any memes that addressed wealth and social class. The majority of those surveyed were left-leaning college students whose algorithms reflected their liberal politics, but even so, out of over a hundred submitted memes, only nine of them took up for the poor. Mould's study found that contemporary leftists were more than happy to call out white "corporate welfare" bros or working-class rural folks on farm subsidies, and that these commentaries were supposed to be progressive as they subverted the stereotype that someone on welfare must be a single mother of color. "The problem was they weren't really doing anything to suggest that *wasn't* the case, all they were doing was adding new people to the definition of 'welfare queen,'" said Mould. "We never got a sympathetic image of somebody who gets assistance from the government." Mould wondered if we have enough counter-proverbs to keep the self-made American Dream narrative in check. "They're surely out there," he told me. "I just don't know that mainstream society has opened up the space to hear them."

Repetition is just one of several linguistic tools that make regurgitating dubious hearsay irresistible. Studies have shown that people perceive information as more believable when presented in easy-to-read fonts and/or easy-to-understand speech styles. A crowd favorite is rhyme. In contemporary studies of the so-called *rhyme-as-reason effect*, researchers found that participants generally rate the phrase "woes unite foes" as more truthful than "woes unite enemies" and "misfortunes unite foes," even though they all mean the same thing. In 1590, Shakespeare penned, "Was there ever any man thus beaten out of season, When in the why and the wherefore is neither rhyme nor reason?"—using the rhyme-as-reason effect itself to note the conflation of artistry and accuracy.

English raconteurs have long used rhyme to ingrain everyday wisdom in listeners' minds.* When I was little, my camp

---

* Rhyme feels extra impactful in English, as opposed to Romance and Slavic languages, like Italian or Russian, in which rhyme appears naturally all the time. English is full of inconsistent word pronunciations, spellings, and verb conjugations, which make rhyming trickier. The language's haphazard political and geographical histories resulted in a hodgepodge of Germanic, Romance, and Celtic. English has thus been called a linguistic "pickpocket," rummaging through the purses of nearby tongues for useful vocabulary. This disorderliness does not lend itself particularly well to organic rhyme. So, what might seem like a corny literary device in French or Greek feels special and satisfying to an English ear. I have often wondered if the English language's chaotic origins inspire a sort of underlying chaos in its speakers.

counselor taught me the phrase "Leaves of three, let it be," so I'd remember what poison ivy looked like and avoid it. In college, I quickly learned "Beer before liquor, you'll never be sicker. Liquor before beer, you're in the clear" (though that tidbit turned out to be demonstrably less reliable). Our brains privilege rhyme in part because it makes language more predictable. In practically every context, unpredictability is disconcerting, so the mind naturally does whatever it can to avoid it. When we encounter a rhyming phrase, we automatically break down the words into sound units called phonemes. This process is called "acoustic encoding," and it's the first step in deciphering any word. With rhyme, the comely sound structure creates a kind of blueprint, a pattern, that seems to make the message itself more sensible. Rhyming "purifies the basics" of our highly complicated world, Harvard psycholinguist Dr. Steven Pinker once said. It brings order to the informational chaos out there. Needless to say, we find this pleasurable.

The same way we enjoy stripes and plaids or a well-arranged kitchen pantry, we are fond of linguistic organization. As Stanford psychologist Barbara Tversky observed, "When thought overwhelms the mind, the mind puts it into the world, notably in diagrams and gestures." The key to memory is finding a nice little place for every thought, and if a statement isn't meaningful enough to feel orderly and thus memorable all on its own, forcing a pattern onto it, like rhyme, will do the trick. Think of catchy political slogans—the Cold War began forty years before I was born, but I know the phrase "Better dead than red" as well as I know "One two buckle my shoe." Unassumingly, rhyme alone works to turn heavy political philosophies into adorable taglines. Like a linguistic halo effect, when an utterance is more attractive, we also take it to be more trustworthy. This is why the rhyme-as-reason rule has also been labeled the "Keats heuristic," referencing the poet John Keats's famed declaration, "Beauty is truth, truth beauty."

Truth, however, is not always the most important goal in storytelling. Instead, it might be to reinforce cultural ideals, demonstrate you're part of an in-group, test social norms, provoke laughter* or disgust, or laughter *and* disgust. Research finds that laughter and disgust are among the emotional responses most likely to make a piece of information both persuasive and shareable.† Laughter and disgust—the exact two reactions my medieval bath story elicited.

I learned from the work of Hunter College psychology professor Tracy Dennis-Tiwary one more reason why so much mythology surrounds the Middle Ages: It was the dawn of modern-day anxiety. In her book *Future Tense: Why Anxiety*

---

* As a genre, jokes do so much more than incite amusement. They allow a speaker to wade through sensitive topics within the safe bounds of plausible deniability. When a joke causes offense, the teller can respond, "I was kidding," and then use that grace to evaluate whether or not the joke really did reflect some internalized prejudice—all without having to admit to a blunder in public. Sometimes, jokes are so clever at camouflaging problematic messaging that tellers themselves don't realize what they've said contradicts their own beliefs. Tom Mould confessed to repeating an old joke about a wealthy woman who brought back a stray dog from a vacation in Mexico, only for the vet to tell her it was actually a large rodent. Mould didn't realize until a friend pointed it out that the joke was xenophobic.

† The others include fear, frustration, and surprise.

Is Good for You (Even Though It Feels Bad), Dennis-Tiwary noted that in medieval Europe, where minds were chained to the Catholic Church and the threat of eternal damnation loomed large, people got used to a certain type of anguish. But starting in the 1500s, as feudalism dissipated and the Scientific Revolution emerged, ideas of agency and selfhood encouraged people to question old ways—to piece together reality's laws and envision a future of possibilities. Psychological troubles then morphed. The motto of the Enlightenment was *Sapere aude*, meaning "dare to know." But Dennis-Tiwary wrote that this new, science-empowered mind that dared to know was also "a vulnerable mind, robbed of the medieval certainty of faith." Budding ideas of self-creation clashed with life's erratic zigzags, and this discord cracked open a geyser of untapped anxiety. "Generations would later call it *existential angst*," Dennis-Tiwary said.

This post-Enlightenment combination of knowledge, angst, and popular sovereignty inspired the West to approach life with a certain style of attack—to conquer both territories and ideas. Ever since, we've carried this bullish attitude toward information with us. During election seasons and other moments of cultural uproar, I find it especially vital to remember that political dogmas become dogmas expressly because they are repeated with fervor. When a politician or pundit starts to sound more like a commercial jingle or broken record than a scholar, that's a cue to listen more closely—to bear in mind that knowledge isn't always meant to go down like a nursery rhyme.

The more I think about the illusory truth effect, the more I think it doesn't work solely on external information, but also on the internal stories we tell ourselves about who we are. I have a personal habit of narrativizing my life so aggressively that it sometimes prevents me from sincerely experiencing it, because I discard any plot points that don't feel on-brand for the genre or trope of my character. My favorite podcast, *Radiolab*, has a riveting episode called "A World Without Words" in which neuroscientist Jill Bolte Taylor is interviewed about her bestselling memoir, *My Stroke of Insight*. The book details the story of a massive stroke Taylor suffered at age thirty-seven, compromising the language centers of her brain. Temporarily, she lost her ability to articulate any thoughts or feelings. At first, losing words sounded like my own customized version of hell, but Taylor said what it actually made her feel was a sense of euphoria, an almost psychedelic oneness with her surroundings. That's because for a few weeks, the mental doctrine she'd been using to self-narrate her life—her archetype, the Freytag's Pyramid of her successes and failures—fell away. Ephemerally, she was a blank slate of pure experience. No repetition, no rhyme. No illusory reason.

    I have spent my life bedeviled by the tug-of-war between awe *and* objectivity, beauty *and* truth. How do we hold both at the same time? This fascination informs the ways I like to learn. My favorite teachers have always been those who are able to paint complex, left-brained ideas with a mythological brush. The late astronomer Carl Sagan was a master of chiseling vivid allegories out of scientific theories: "We're made of star stuff"; "If you wish to make an apple pie from scratch, you must first invent the universe."

Moiya McTier's work lives precisely at the intersection of physics and folklore. McTier was raised in the 1990s and early 2000s in Pennsylvania's dense woods in a cabin with no electricity or running water—just her imagination and a clear view of the stars. McTier went on to become the first Harvard graduate in history to double-major in astrophysics and mythology, as well as the first Black woman to earn a PhD in astronomy from Columbia University. "I think my study of folklore has given me a flexibility where I understand that there are different epistemologies," she told me. "There are different foundations of truth that you can operate on at different times." When McTier is hired to give a public science lecture or consult on a film where the writers want to ensure a physics plot point makes sense, she acknowledges that sometimes hard, fixed data is not the most effective way to communicate. "Sometimes people need something more empathetic or more abstract," she said.

Tom Mould explained that while memorable phrasing might not make information more accurate, it does make it more powerful because of how "transportable" language is. "They say stories transport people into the story world, but also, narratives are incredibly transportable themselves," he said. You can easily tote along catchy proverbs like "woes unite foes" or "haters are my motivators" and use them in all kinds of situations, like a semantic Swiss Army knife. Stories work the same way. "You can rip a story out of its context and retell it in other places," said Mould. You can't do this with stats, graphs, and charts—forms of data often helmed as universally superior. "It's hard to remember a graph," Mould continued. "But what if I told you about an experiment in the form of a story?" Mistaking an anecdote for an objective fact is dubious, but using a story to breathe life into an objective fact is nothing short of magic.

Different scientific fields use the language of mythology to convey their concepts all the time. In her biochemistry research, my mother conceived the term "anastasis," Greek for "resurrection," to describe cells recovering from the brink of death. I'm fond as well of the term "Goldilocks Zone," astronomy's nickname for the planetary temperature conditions conducive to life. (Both dazzling and thoroughly true, earth finds itself smack dab in the middle of our solar system's Goldilocks Zone.) Before her untimely passing in 1999 from the same lymphoma my mom later had, astronomer Rebecca Elson published a poetry collection called *A Responsibility to Awe*, which contains a collage of spectacular science symbolism made even more gorgeous by its accuracy: "If the ocean is like the universe, then the waves are stars." "We astronomers are nomads . . . all the earth our tent."

NINE

SORRY I'M LATE, MUST BE MERCURY IN RETROGRADE
A note on confirmation bias

Some people have meditation, some people have Jesus Christ, but lately, the only thing that cures my existential dread is dinosaurs. Devouring dinosaur YouTube videos, ogling fossils at natural history museums, even just sitting around thinking about baby theropods following their moms across Pangea. Dinosaurs give me that sense of awe we're supposed to feel. Anytime I gush about Velociraptors and Iguanodons in casual conversation, people tend to assume I'm on psychedelics, but I hope I never come down from the thrill of knowing that spectacular earth aliens reigned over this planet for 174 million years, long before humans—who've been here for only .01 percent of that time—were ever a twinkle in evolution's eye. If you think of life as a fancy house party and earth as the house, it was dinosaurs who threw this shindig 245 million years ago. They got evicted undeservedly after epochs of immaculate tenancy, and we humans are the little punks who just showed up and think we own the place. Dinosaurs kept this house pristine, and now we're trashing it, soaking the furniture in cheap beer, shattering ceramic keepsakes, and puking in the pool. *We're* the ones who deserve eviction. If you don't start composting for the sake of future generations, I say do it in loving memory of the dinosaurs.

The day after the Supreme Court overturned *Roe v. Wade* in 2022, I went to an animatronic dinosaur exhibit. It couldn't have been a more perfect diversion. A new pal of mine, Kristen, had been besieged by Instagram ads for the attraction, which was located on a hot slab of suburb forty minutes outside of L.A. At long last, she surrendered to a promo deal and invited me, having made my Mesozoic obsession known early in our friendship, to tag along. Amid a spattering of elementary schoolers and their dads, Kristen and I promenaded through the dark warehouse, lined with several dozen reptilian replicas ranging in size from motorcycles to small yachts. Each bathed in an LED rainbow glow, the dinos hissed, pawed the ground, and waggled their mighty jaws at regularly timed intervals. Like little girls at Disneyland, Kristen and I gasped at their amber eyeballs and curvaceous head adornments, then devoured each placard's stats: "How the fuck did they figure out their maximum running speeds?" "Ooh, I think I found the one with the tiniest arms."* "Aw, look at the baby Parasaurolophus!"

---

* The T. rex is known for sporting arms of irregular tininess, but they were actually a full meter long. Built for slashing prey, they could lift an estimated four hundred pounds each. Still, silly looking.

Wonkily proportioned and jury-rigged as they were, the animatronics poured a soothing dose of calamine lotion on a nasty rash of a week. They were a welcome reminder of the ephemerality of tragedy: Lusher days (and who knows? Maybe a species-ending asteroid) no doubt lay ahead. Corny jokes were made about how our Supreme Court was full of beasts more primordial than this exhibit; temporary T. rex tattoos were purchased at the gift shop and blithely applied to upper breasts and lower backs in the bathroom.

Kristen grew up in a conservative evangelical community outside Dallas, Texas, whose members believed in neither abortion nor paleontology. A mermaid-haired bisexual with dreams of becoming a cinema star, Kristen escaped at twenty-two to Los Angeles, where she replaced the Jesus-centric rituals of her past with astrology and *The L Word* watch parties. Ex-evangelical theater kids are some of my favorite people to befriend. Their cinematic hell-themed trauma gives them an absurdist sense of humor that jibes oddly well with my culturally Jewish cynicism. Their anecdotes of "prayer therapy" and speaking in tongues are more exotic and gripping to me than any true-crime podcast.

As we meandered past a family of mechanical herbivores, Kristen told me about her fundamentalist middle school, where she learned dinosaurs lived only two thousand years ago and cohabitated with Adam and Eve. "We were taught that God didn't let them on Noah's Ark—that's why they went extinct," she confessed, fiddling with a strand of fake ivy suspended from the ceiling. "Well, that's not very fair,"

I responded. "God let mosquitoes in, but not dinos? What'd they ever do to him?" "I don't think they explained that far," said Kristen, then snapped a portrait of a mewing Triceratops.

When fossil hunters started uncovering prehistoric skeletons in heaps during the so-called Bone Wars of the nineteenth century, inerrant Christians like Kristen's ancestors freaked out. They worked backwards from their conclusions about Genesis to make these discoveries line up. The bones were God testing their faith. Or maybe they were just decorative, like holy subdermal implants. I can't imagine the cognitive dissonance those people must have felt. Sounds far more exhausting in the long run than just admitting you might've been wrong.

Actually, though . . . I *can* imagine the dissonance. It's the same kind of sickening internal skirmish I feel about myself all the time. Most of us gape, aghast, at the actions of religious fanatics, wolfish tech CEOs, and oppressive Supreme Court justices. "How do they sleep at night?" we ask ourselves. The explanation is simple—just how all of us do. Daily, I engage in behaviors I later regret or never stood by in the first place. I've texted while driving, talked smack behind people's backs, and doubled down on arguments I knew in the moment were bullshit. I've bought fast fashion made by exploited overseas factory workers and voluntarily watched movies made by known predators. Conveniently, I've also performed the mental contortionism necessary to justify every single last one of these choices to myself. I sleep at night like a swaddled infant. I've embraced evidence that

I'm a profoundly good person and dismissed all feedback to the contrary. The stakes might not be Supreme Court–level high, but my zigzag toward rationalization takes a nearly identical shape. This cognitive acrobatic act is known as *confirmation bias*.

Confirmation bias has crept into mainstream discourse like a sleeper hit indie song, thanks to analyses of our ever-intensifying political divides—and the role of algorithmic newsfeeds in entrenching users' beliefs and dehumanizing their opponents. Broadly, the bias is characterized by a universal tendency to favor information that validates our existing views and discard that which refutes them. It's an ancient heuristic that oozes into nearly every decision a person might make, from macro-level political ideologies to minor daily character assessments (say, swiping left on a potential date because they're a Scorpio, and we *all* know how Scorpios can be. Kidding. Or am I?).

Theoretically, there is no psychological scenario too outlandish or high-risk for confirmation bias. It has the power to make a person self-justify nearly any crime or irrationality, from Mafia bosses committing murder to conspiratorial zealots detecting "proof" of their convictions everywhere they look, decoding hidden messages where there are none. When you start with a conclusion that's difficult or impossible to prove (say, "The earth is only two thousand years old," or "I don't get along with Scorpios"), confirmation bias is the crooked detective helping you work backwards to find the right clues. The bias is like one of those hydraulic presses that can crush even a bowling ball—only the rarest, hardiest, most perfectly shaped truths have any hope of resisting.

Confirmation bias was the very first cognitive bias I learned about. It came up in much of my *Cultish* research. For that book, I was specifically investigating techniques of cult language—linguistic tactics that any power-hungry leader can weaponize, not just black-robed satanists, but also politicians, corporate figureheads, even pop stars. The linguistics made sense to me, but I was having trouble with the psychology. How could a relatively intelligent, discerning person bring themselves to stick with a group, even after losing everything, including a foundational sense of who they are? Confirmation bias proved a significant part of the answer. When you've come to believe something is true but are presented with contrary facts, the brain naturally does whatever it takes to unsee or reinterpret them.

One of my favorite books on confirmation bias is 2007's *Mistakes Were Made (But Not by Me)*. In it, authors Tavris and Aronson cite a study from the early 2000s where participants were hooked up to MRIs and presented with data that either emboldened or negated their pre-held views on George W. Bush and John Kerry. Faced with facts they didn't like, the reasoning areas of participants' brains went dark, as if the prefrontal cortex stuck its fingers in its ears, shouted *lalala,* and left the room. By contrast, when shown corroborative information, their minds' emotional provinces lit up brighter than my smile at the dinosaur exhibit. A canon of studies has replicated this finding that facts disproving one's stance are not only unconvincing, they make a person dig in harder. It's been termed the "backfire effect." Not even the smartest, most scrupulous people are immune. Once you've committed to an idea and defended its prudence, adjusting your mental framework to new data is much harder than just ignoring it, or shoehorning it in and performing whatever psychological Pilates will make it stick.

I found this information personally humbling. Confirmation bias explained not only the choices of Jonestown followers and modern political extremists for whom facts made no difference, but also scores of my own bizarre choices. Several years into my relationship with Mr. Backpack, during a period of peak unpleasantness, I spent an evening taking internet quiz after internet quiz to determine whether or not we should break up. Only one result produced a "no." Guess which one I listened to. My decision-making strategy was like shaking a Magic 8 Ball and only stopping once I landed on an answer that reinforced a decision I'd already made. "Without a doubt," shake, "Signs point to yes," shake, "Reply hazy, try again," shake . . .

After Kristen and I finished up at the dinosaur exhibit, she suggested we do as the suburbanites do and enjoy happy hour at Chili's. A fond memory of the chain restaurant's early-2000s commercial jingle enveloped my temporal lobe like the smell of an old lover's hair: *I want my baby back, baby back, baby back* . . . A cheap, nostalgia-laced margarita and some queso sounded like exactly the soul medicine I needed. In the last year, cocktail prices in Los Angeles had crept up to an offensive $18. And for what, atmosphere? Barstools had gotten so jawbreaker-hard, mood lighting so dark, and shoegaze music so loud that if I hadn't already committed to the lifestyle, I might actually see it as torture. "Chili's is perfect," I replied.

Over $6 blackberry margaritas the size of our faces, Kristen and I plunged back into comparing sagas from our upbringings. Where she grew up in Texas, everyone lived in daily anticipation of the Rapture. At any moment, Jesus could rise again and bring along only his true loyalists to the candy-coated amusement park of heaven. Everyone else would be left behind to burn. So you better accept Him into your heart every day, and with feeling, or you'd be doomed just like the dinosaurs.

As concepts, confirmation bias and the apocalypse are an exquisite pairing. I've come to believe the mind is built for doomsday. So many phenomena can feel like "proof" that the sky is falling, from a species-ending asteroid to the threat of imminent layoffs. Losing an AirPod can feel like dystopia. A bout of bad weather can feel like dystopia. In *Slouching Towards Bethlehem*, Didion called L.A.'s Santa Ana winds "the weather of catastrophe." She said the winds' "violence and the unpredictability . . . affect the entire quality of life in Los Angeles, accentuate its impermanence, its unreliability. The winds show us how close to the edge we are." On any scale, instability can make a person feel like the world really is ending, even when it's not, like, not even close. I find it peculiar that as scientific explanations for things like heavy wind become both more accurate and easier to understand, our sense of doomsday doesn't disappear. Clearly, more information doesn't fix the agitation. If you want evidence that the apocalypse is nigh, confirmation bias will ensure that you find it.

The first time I ever personally contemplated the end of the world was in 1999. I was swinging on my backpack one morning before school, when I overheard a voice on the radio say that something called "Y2K" was coming and had more than a few people convinced that the clocks, computers, and banks were going to shut down. Something called "anarchy" was predicted to ensue. These believers—"doomers," they called themselves—were cashing in their retirement accounts and selling their stock holdings, hoarding beans and rice by the metric ton. My parents didn't seem worried about this end-times business, and neither did the lady on NPR, so I figured Y2K was just another folk tale, like the Bogeyman or the Loch Ness Monster,* and some grown-ups were just a little too scared.

---

* The mass discovery and display of dinosaur bones in the nineteenth century swayed people's perceptions of the Loch Ness Monster. Before dinosaurs were in movies and on children's bedsheets, whenever someone claimed to have spotted a marine beast, they reported it looked like a snake. Then, as dinosaur awareness increased, sighters' descriptions started more closely resembling Mesozoic sea reptiles, like the Plesiosaurus—a finned, long-necked dinosaur that looks *exactly* like my personal image of Nessie. New knowledge didn't quell fears of mythical beasts, it simply reshaped them.

Indeed, Y2K came and went, and the world didn't stop... but neither did the doomers.* Flooded with cognitive dissonance, they had two options: either admit everything they'd done was ridiculous, or go for broke. There was no debate. Confirmation bias was their Ark, and the majority of doomers clung to it, upholding that their Y2K preparations weren't absurd, there was proof all around that they'd been right. Message boards teemed with testimonies of malfunctioning VCRs and ATMs. Even the lack of evidence was interpreted as evidence, a sure sign of government cover-up. Doomers who admitted they'd been mistaken were decried as dunces and traitors. "Despite family and friends laughing at me and telling me I was crazy for preparing, I persevered and prepared anyway. Now I am TOTALLY EMBARRASSED," posted one rogue user to a forum shortly after the new year. His comment was immediately hounded with vitriol from other survivalists, handling their dissonance the opposite way. "A genuine Y2K-aware-prepper would never make such idiotic statements," replied one user of many, more certain than ever that the cataclysm for which they'd planned and canned was imminent. And honestly? 9/11, the 2008 economic recession, COVID-19. The apocalypse, they could argue, *did* come.

---

* Two decades after Y2K, doomers still exist but have since rebranded as "preppers." On Amazon, prepper kits are a robust category: Within the week, you could have a bucket of eighty-four shelf-stable emergency meals delivered for $160 (which sounds just plain economical to me, apocalypse or not).

How's this for seeing only what you want to see: In sun-drenched, dream-big Southern California, blaming technological mishaps on a cosmic conspiracy is in fact a beloved custom. Here, we call it astrology. Earnestly, ironically, or some mix of the two, high-functioning adults in Los Angeles commonly call upon zodiac signs and retrograde star positions to excuse indiscretions from missed appointments to poor texting etiquette. "Sorry I'm late, classic Pisces vibes!" is a statement I overheard not twenty-four hours ago. Charts and horoscopes are exchanged ritualistically at every social affair. Once, in the midst of a horrendous professional tribulation, one of my dear friends attempted to console me by blaming my "Saturn return"—the celestial pattern said to yield major life changes around the age of twenty-nine. At a house party last year, a fellow guest announced with stars in her eyes that she had an auspicious feeling her current creative project was going to take off because a TikTok astrologer told her so. She rolled me the clip: "If you're seeing this on your For You Page, it was *meant* to find you. You are about to manifest abundance!" a boho-chic woman with eyelash extensions crooned in exchange for over 200,000 likes. It's simply a wise engagement strategy—harness onlookers' confirmation biases in bulk by telling everyone who thumbs past your content exactly what they want to hear.

Of course, confirmation bias serves a purpose, or else it wouldn't exist. In a 2020 paper, German philosopher Uwe Peters noted that one of the bias's evolutionary benefits might be that "it helps us bring social reality into alignment with our beliefs." How unsustainably chaotic would it feel if our social reality and beliefs never synced up? When approached with a skeptical wink, "Saturn return" is a lens through which to bond over a shared pattern: the quarter-life crisis. It's lovely to have excuses to connect with each other, to ignore one another's differences because you have something in common, even if that something is mostly made-up.

If confirmation bias didn't exist at all, we'd agonize over every choice: Should I order a salad or fries? Should I accept that job or wait for a better one? Why didn't we break up before things got bad? Why didn't I spend more time with my grandparents? Why didn't I invest in Zoom in 2019, get rich, and put an offer on that fabulous Zillow listing right before the market inflated and officially screwed me forever? "Confirmation bias helps you get rid of the type of uncertainty that could hold a person back from making a timely decision," Knox College psychologist Frank McAndrew told me. The bias lets us live with ourselves.

But what if accuracy is important and timeliness isn't? Like in political or financial scenarios, or interpersonal dilemmas involving a bevy of emotional variables? This appears to be one of confirmation bias's greatest threats—it offers the mind blanket permission to oversimplify arguments in an age when arguments are only getting thornier. This blunting of ideas intensifies us-vs.-them divisions in a social climate that demands we learn to tolerate the mental toll of cognitive dissonance, not hydraulic-press it into oblivion, if we don't want our mental levees to break and our biases to flood in all at once. McAndrew explained, "If an issue requires slow thinking, well, you not only have confirmation bias to worry about but when you start to look at what the other side is saying, now you're in competition with them. Now, zero sum bias starts to kick in, because you want to be more right than they are. All of these things are operating at one time. It's very rare that a mistake happens because of just one bias."

I learned in my cult reporting that whether we're discussing political partisans, astrology lovers, evangelicals, doomsday preppers, or Taylor Swift stans, a sense of social belonging is more valuable than any one given belief. And it's certainly more valuable than the truth. Confirmation bias works overtime in ideologically bound groups, where questioning a tenet (like the story of Genesis, or Taylor Swift's genius) would mean betraying an identity, an aesthetic, a sisterhood. If changing your mind means losing your "tribe," it's not worth it. A classic 1979 Stanford study found that after confronting equally compelling evidence that either supported or refuted capital punishment, participants reported feeling even more attached to their original views on the matter. A 2011 Yale experiment on climate change perceptions concluded that becoming *more* scientifically literate actually made study subjects *less* willing to entertain the opposing side. Why? Additional information just made them better at defending their credo. "Cultural polarization actually gets bigger, not smaller, as science literacy and numeracy increase," concluded the researchers. "As ordinary members of the public learn more about science . . . they become more skillful in seeking out and making sense of—or if necessary explaining away—empirical evidence relating to their groups' positions."

In her prescient postapocalyptic novel *Station Eleven*, author Emily St. John Mandel included a scene where a group of people from all backgrounds watched a television anchor break the news that a worldwide pandemic had hit, and all the onlookers actually believed him. I met Mandel at a literary festival in 2022, six years after *Station Eleven* was published, when she divulged that this news anchor scene now seemed implausible. No longer could we expect a group of random pedestrians to tune in to the same broadcast and all hear the same thing. "We've lost consensual reality, and I don't know how we get that back. It's like a menu now—choose your own reality," said Mandel.

If beliefs are less important than belonging, what, then, if it were culturally permissible to interrogate a belief at any time? What if a desire to seek actual facts weren't seen as such a betrayal, and a certain thinker being right about one thing didn't make another wrong about everything?

As a general and frustrating rule, using facts to try and force another person's mind to change is not always, as a behavioral economist might say, a rational use of one's limited time and cognitive resources. Fortunately, though, we do have pretty good luck changing our own minds. A 2021 study published in *Philosophical Transactions of the Royal Society* found that when people trained themselves to notice their own thought processes, they were able to strengthen their defenses against misinformation and dogma. I am still nursing this talent; I'm certain I won't ever master it. But the ongoing challenge has made me, if nothing else, more compassionate toward others' irrationalities and skeptical of my own.

In her book *The Extended Mind*, science writer Annie Murphy Paul illustrates the love–hate relationship many of us have with our own minds. "We often regard the brain as an organ of awesome and almost unfathomable power. But we're also apt to treat it with high-handed imperiousness, expecting it to do our bidding as if it were a docile servant," she writes. "Pay attention to this, we tell it; remember that; buckle down now and get the job done. Alas, we often find that the brain is . . . fickle in its focus, porous in its memory, and inconstant in its efforts."

I have lost untold hours overanalyzing the world to death. I have spent thousands in therapy teasing out other people's confounding choices, futilely attempting to intellectualize my way out of misery, as if the perfect rationalization for why someone acted a certain way would cause their behavior to change and my soul to heal. I will always believe in the material power of words and facts, but I also know there's a point past which they don't make you feel any better. The emotional burden of too much information can't always be quelled by more information.

When the volume in my brain gets too high, I find my way back to dinosaurs. More honest than any cyclical thought, they put things into perspective. Kristen and I learned at the animatronic exhibit that the word "dinosaur" was hatched in 1842 by a British naturalist named Sir Richard Owen. With Greek roots, the term translates to "terrible lizard." For more than a century, scientists thought dinosaurs all looked like monsters. But the more they unearthed of them, the less terrible and lizardish they seemed. Dinosaurs weren't just scaly green Godzillas. There were thousands of diverse species, some with feathers like a peacock's and others as diminutive in size as cocker spaniels. Dinosaurs were sometimes gorgeous, sometimes fearsome, and incalculable details about them are lost to time. I prefer this version of their story. It's an allegory—I can stick with the uncomplicated conclusion that the world is full of beasts, or I can retrieve my brush and bit by bit, start sweeping away the debris. The world can be so humbling, but only if you let it humble you.

TEN

NOSTALGIA PORN
A note on declinism

In his discussions of flow states, Mihaly Csikszentmihalyi pointed out that since the 1950s, the percentage of Americans who report their life is "very happy" has gone basically unchanged. When I shared this stat with Casey, he responded with surprise. "It's just, the overall quality of life has gone up so much since then. Like, exponentially," he said.

More startling to me was the number itself. Casey guessed this "very happy" percentage was around 33. I'd have predicted somewhere closer to 15 percent (shows my attitude). But he was right. Aside from a brief dip in 2021, the percentage of self-reported super-content Americans has hung around 30 percent. We've indeed come a long way since the 1950s; people are living longer and hurtling toward more opportunity and convenience than ever. But collectively, we don't seem to be getting happier. There's something about that emotional calculus that doesn't check out. If we're making exponential "progress" but not feeling better, then what, one might ask, is the point? This stat doesn't exactly inspire hope for the future. But you know what does? Nostalgia for the past.

My favorite neologism of the century so far is "anemoia," which describes the feeling of nostalgia for a time you've never known. The term was coined by John Koenig, author of *The Dictionary of Obscure Sorrows*, an enchanting compendium of imagined words for previously unnamed emotions. Like "looseleft," the feeling of loss after finishing a good book, or "rubatosis," the disquieting awareness of your own heartbeat. "Anemoia" references two words from Ancient Greek: *ánemos*, meaning "wind," and *nóos*, meaning "mind." It was the perfect language to borrow from, I think, since Ancient Greece has long been romanticized in the very spirit of anemoia. Even Ancient Greeks themselves must have glamorized certain bygone eras—perhaps Ancient Egypt for its egalitarian attitudes, or the hunter-gatherers for their transcendentalism. Nostalgia is a timeless feeling, though it certainly has its collective spikes, periods when civilization feels like it's changing too quickly. People get overwhelmed by the present and disappear into the past. Ancient Greece saw the whole Bronze Age. It saw the invention of the city-state, the Olympics, cartography, geometry, philosophy. So much, so fast. I can easily see how the Ancient Greeks, like us right now, might have craved simpler times they never knew. Anemoia.

Idealizing the far-off past, while very much enjoying the modern comforts of the present, has become a curious cultural pattern. I've watched tradwives* on Instagram hand-dyeing nineteenth-century-style prairie dresses in front of anamorphic iPhone lenses. I've patronized Etsy's extensive "cottagecore" category, thousands of modern products optimized for nostalgia: "magical mushroom LED night light," "curated gift box of vintage curiosities." In the thick of the pandemic, I spent $32 to have a lady in rural Vermont ship me a grab bag of ostrich feathers, crocodile teeth, petrified wood, and a pocket-size herbology booklet so I could cosplay a Victorian forest sprite. Maybe the more anxiety-provoking the current moment, the further back in time we feel the need to go. Nostalgia softens an era's harsh edges, so we can sink back into a warm bath of fantasy. Novelist Ursula K. Le Guin wrote in *Tales from Earthsea*, "Past events exist, after all, only in memory, which is a form of imagination. The event is real now, but once it's then, its continuing reality is entirely up to us, dependent on our energy and honesty." Maintaining honesty about the past is so exhausting, many of us opt not to try.

I'm a sucker for anemoia, personally. Call it escapism or outright denial, but I've spent the past few years adorning my

---

* Short for "traditional wife," tradwives are a contingent of twenty-first-century women who choose to kick it old-school by assuming normatively feminine responsibilities like cooking, gardening, tidying, and rearing children. My favorite kind of tradwife takes style notes from Laura Ingalls Wilder and Snow White: floral peasant dresses, flouncy aprons. Sort of an anti-Kardashian, the tradwife is not a #bossbabe. She is too busy preserving figs and folding linens to worry about conquering the world.

house in vintage toadstool tchotchkes and writing periodically by candlelight, as if I'm a spinster in the French countryside, or maybe a Manson girl living on L.A.'s dusty Spahn Ranch before the shit hit the fan. I've cherry-picked my own oddities box of erstwhile practices, focusing on the best of every era I've never known to avoid facing the worst of this one. It might make more sense during times of discomfort to dream about the future since that's actually where we're headed, but the future is unknown, unsettling. The future doesn't have any tangible artifacts—no prairie dresses, no vinyl records. Most of us would rather experience something familiar, even if negative, than take a chance on the unknown.

Nostalgia is an affective quirk, but it has a cognitive analog. Plenty of everyday moods pair with a respective bias. Envy, for example, is to zero-sum bias as paranoia is to proportionality bias as nostalgia is to *declinism*—the false impression that things are worse now than they were in the past, and it's all downhill from here.

Cognitive psychology research has revealed that memories of negative emotions dwindle quicker than the positive,[*] a phenomenon known as the *fading affect bias*. Because most of us prefer reminiscing about happy times, our cheery revisions grow stronger, while bad memories wither away, leading to a general idealization of the past. Declinism explains why one might thumb through old photos of themselves,

---

[*] Memories of traumatic events, which can stalk a rememberer in involuntary flashbacks, are notable exceptions.

longing to be nineteen and baby-cheeked again, even if they know that age felt miserable and directionless in the moment.

In my own life, declinism shows up mostly in daydreams, when work obligations feel so overwhelming that I start to consider trading my apartment in Los Angeles for a remote cabin and my synthetic sweatsuit for a bell-shaped crinoline petticoat to live like it's 1849 again—never mind that everyone was dying of tuberculosis then, and women had no rights. In 2023, I saw the poet and memoirist Maggie Nelson speak on book tour for her essay collection *On Freedom*, where she addressed the trend of feminists turned tradwives. She suggested that the phenomenon of progressives-gone-*Little House in the Big Woods* might have emerged from a generation of women feeling like they were promised a kind of liberation that didn't pan out as they hoped, so they decided to swing back into a form of aesthetically updated Puritanism. Plus, they had the spare resources to opt into a more laborious lifestyle, hand-making their own oat milk and all. In the process, they wound up running into a demographic of right-wing antifeminists who arrived in the farmhouse kitchen for different reasons, darker reasons, but that's horseshoe theory for you. Declinism gives us psychological as well as cultural permission to normalize the belief that life was inarguably better or at least more spiritually bearable in the "good old days," whenever those were.

The brain is perennially odd about time. It defaults to hyper-dramatizing the present, glorifying the past, and devaluing the future. Related to declinism, a deception labeled *present bias* describes our propensity to blow out of proportion events that are currently happening while undervaluing what will come in a few years or even days. A 2015 UCLA psychology study found that people conceive of their future selves as strangers, which is why we often procrastinate our homework and put off saving for retirement. We find it hard to care about those random nobodies, even though they're our soon-to-be selves.

Coco Mellors, author of the novel *Blue Sisters*, hates nostalgia. She got sober about a decade ago and harbors little sentimentality for the years prior. "Nostalgia feels dishonest," she told me. "The past is inherently conflicted and nuanced, but nostalgia reduces it to its most benign." I agree that reminiscing, or dwelling if you prefer, can turn maudlin and self-destructive. It certainly doesn't jibe with the "one day at a time" ethos of recovery. Mellors went on, "As an addict, it's dangerous to look back and remember your greatest hits—that night you drank exactly the right amount and were charming and funny—because that was never the reality. You have to remember what those times were really like in order to remember why you don't want to go back."

Romanticizing the past can have an odd tempering effect on art, too. Throughout the sociopolitical upheavals of the late 2010s and early 2020s, Hollywood comfort-fed us a buffet of nostalgic jaunts down memory lane: The casts of *Friends* and *Harry Potter* reassembled for tearful reunion specials. Disney turned its canon of animated classics into a cash cow of live-action remakes (2019's freaky CGI version of *Lady and the Tramp* continues to haunt me). TV "rewatch" podcasts, where former costars of *The Office* and *The O.C.* rehashed on-set memories, launched by the dozen. In COVID quarantine, I lost myself in a swirl of insipid cinematic reboots, whose titles I won't betray because I loved them despite their mediocrity—or maybe because of it.

Sociologist Tressie McMillan Cottom said, "Nostalgic celebrity is a neutered artist. We like that." These remakes were, as Cottom pointed out, apolitical, shallow, and comforting. Who wants to be challenged by something they're explicitly seeking out for warm fuzzies? "Nostalgia blunts the politics that produces all art, especially middlebrow art," wrote Cottom. Would Disneyland still be the most magical place on earth if we acknowledged that the park was originally built to offer lily-white suburbanites a shrine away from the urban racial and sexual upheavals of the mid-century? Cottom's comments were specifically directed at the culture's renewed embrace of Dolly Parton for a 2021 essay titled "The Dolly Moment: Why We Stan a Post Racism Queen." She wrote, "Even if you remember that *9 to 5* was part of a mainstreaming of big-tent working-woman feminism, you cannot feel the urgency of the time. . . . There is no petition to sign, no march to attend and fight to be had about whether women belong in the workplace."

Nostalgia shamelessly revises our attitudes toward public figures. I think of the triumphant comeback stories of celebrity bombshells like Britney Spears, Paris Hilton, Lindsay Lohan, and Pamela Anderson. During my Y2K adolescence, the tabloid-driven consensus was that these women were has-beens and harlots; but less than fifteen years later, they each experienced a stunning, synchronized career resurgence, awarded Broadway stardom, Netflix movie deals, and emancipation. Come 2020, these formerly tyrannized figures weren't viewed as bimbos single-handedly ruining wholesome American femininity but instead undervalued angels, sights for sore eyes. As soon as the pandemic hit and cravings for the "Great Before" spiked, Pam and Paris served a once-ruthless mob mashed-potato comfort, like when you run into a former high school nemesis but feel all sweet and sentimental for old times' sake. I don't credit feminism for audiences' reassessment of these women. I chalk it up to nostalgia.

Weaponizing delusions of the past is an age-old populist marketing tactic—both a political campaign ploy and capitalist tool. Where revisionist history is concerned, declinism arguably does its dirtiest work during election seasons, when candidates blur history's sharp corners to radicalize a restless public and win their votes. Far-right nationalists are known to harken back to their country's supposed "Golden Age," hiding xenophobic and exclusionary policies under the promise of restoring the nation to its former glory. France's ultraconservative National Rally party has long romanticized its colonial history, backing policies that prioritize the interests of native-born French citizens over immigrants and refugees. The far-right Alternative for Germany party has downplayed the atrocities of the Nazi regime, calling for stricter immigration policies, while stoking fear and resentment toward outsiders. During the Nazis' initial rise to power, Hitler used the slogan "Make Germany Great Again," which may sound more freshly familiar. For generations, politicians have cashed in on the narrative that their nation once enjoyed a time of utopian prosperity and that only their agenda, brutal or not, will work to reinstate it.

The world *is* declining in at least one significant way—the climate crisis, which outshines so many other issues that are actually improving, like clean water and education. Failing to "focus on the positive" in the face of an ongoing global disaster makes intuitive sense. But even when challenges are objectively small, like a misplaced sweater or snippy email from a coworker, they have the capacity to feel equally stressful. For this, we can partially thank *negativity bias*—the tendency to assign greater weight to unfavorable events. We internalize the scorch of rebuke much more powerfully than the warm glow of praise. A slap in the face will likely have a stronger short-term impact than a hug. That we could receive a hundred genuine compliments but register only the backhanded outlier might have an adaptive explanation: An insult in a litany of compliments is today's rattlesnake in a field of flowers. Learning to ignore a meadow of pleasant magnolias in order to zero in on the deadly snake (even if it turned out just to be a stick) had survival benefits, and evolutionary habits die hard. Primed to hyper-fixate on present negativity while glossing over the distant past, we naturally landed at declinism.

Declinism predicts that every generation will remain convinced that life is only getting worse. Outstandingly, differently worse. I notice it in language. Since the Trump presidency, I've heard talk of doomsday trickle its way from fringe message boards into quotidian pleasantries. In my community of well-cushioned Californians, opening a conversation with "How are you? I mean, aside from the world burning and all" is practically good manners. *The world is burning, everything sucks, doomsday vibes.* Fatalistic hyperbole has gone trendy vernacular. I, too, have invoked the end of the world in casual conversation, even though the earth is still very much beneath my feet, and I don't find it helpful to act like it's not. I have to wonder if there's any danger to this deadening of our emotional vocabularies. What does it do to us to overuse this defeatist rhetoric, perhaps only ironically at first, but then so cavalierly and with such frequency that one day we forget it's not earnest, each of us the boy who cried apocalypse? Sometimes it seems like people almost *want* the end of the world to show up already, like addicts who pray to hit rock bottom so at least they know it can't get worse.

The attitude that things used to be nice, are currently shit, and will keep on trending downward might carry a certain blasé neoliberal cachet, but it risks self-fulfilling prophecy. Agreeing that the world is burning and there's nothing to be done means giving permission to engage in behaviors that stoke the flame. In his 2012 coauthored book, *Catastrophism*, Eddie Yuen wrote about "catastrophe fatigue" in the context of climate activism. "The ubiquity of apocalypse in recent decades has led to a banalization of the concept—it is seen as normal, expected, in a sense comfortable," he said. It's mordant timing that the mainstreaming of dystopia everywhere from TV series to small talk has come to serve as a perverse pacifier, an excuse for inertia, exactly "as the contours of the multipronged environmental crisis are coming into sharp focus." Now, said Yuen, scientists with their measured action items are having to "compete in this marketplace of catastrophe" in order to be heard. John Koenig might categorize catastrophe fatigue as a "wytai," defined in *The Dictionary of Obscure Sorrows* as "a feature of modern society that suddenly strikes you as absurd and grotesque."

In 2016, Oxford economist and philosopher Max Roser wrote a piece for *Vox* titled "Proof That Life Is Getting Better for Humanity, in 5 Charts." He wrote, "The media . . . does not nearly pay enough attention to the slow developments that reshape our world." Most people think world poverty is on the rise, but surveys show it's been dropping exponentially for decades. "Newspapers could (and should) have run this headline every single day since 1990 . . . 'The number of people in extreme poverty fell by 130,000 since yesterday,'" said Roser. No time has ever been better for literacy or civil liberty, fertility or life expectancy. My mother swears the cure for cancer is just around the corner. More people than ever can access infinite knowledge in seconds, and with practice, they can even hope to remember some of it. They can have psilocybin chocolates delivered to their front doors in time for their appointment at the Getty. Regarding her hopes for the feminist movement, Maggie Nelson said on her 2023 book tour, "I'm an optimist! So sue me." She quoted James Baldwin, who declared sixty years earlier, "I can't be a pessimist because I am alive. To be a pessimist means that you have agreed that human life is an academic matter."

I continue to marvel, though, that we can peruse chart after chart illustrating how much better life is now than it was in the past and still feel in our animal bodies that the opposite is true. Some of this intuitive dissonance may spring from Csikszentmihalyi's observation that while wealth and overall quality of life may be improving, happiness is not. Accounting for inflation, median household incomes more than doubled in the U.S. between the 1950s and 2020s—but unless someone went from below the poverty line to above it, their happiness didn't necessarily budge. "You can find that the lack of basic resources . . . contributes to unhappiness, but the increase in material resources [does] not increase happiness," said Csikszentmihalyi.

Freedom, conversely, tells a different story than money. It's hard to OD on freedom. Generally, the more one has, the happier they'll be[*]—all kinds of freedoms, including speech, thought, bodily autonomy, and I have to believe freedom from

---

[*] In the U.S., happiness gradually increased among marginalized populations (albeit with a lag) after the gender and civil rights movements awarded them more liberties. Currently, the demographic with the bleakest outlook is less-than-college-educated white men. According to Carol Graham, a Brookings researcher and public policy professor at the University of Maryland College Park, out-of-work white men are "overrepresented in the crisis of deaths of despair" (suicide, drug overdose, liver disease). Financial hardship does not explain this despair; studies find that when women lose their jobs, they aren't as negatively affected.

consumerism. In his book *Sedated: How Modern Capitalism Created Our Mental Health Crisis*, medical anthropologist James Davies noted that when our basic human needs for safety, economic stability, loving connection, authenticity, and meaningful work are neglected, materialism is usually offered as a quick, duplicitous fix—"a culturally endorsed coping mechanism that ultimately backfired." Perhaps our anemoia for "simpler," less consumerist times helps us generate hope for a simpler, less consumerist future.

Brain scans show that when we think back on pleasant memories, the same cranial regions light up as when we daydream about days to come. No wonder I've been so into dinosaurs, cottagecore, and Harry Potter reunions. Perhaps we shouldn't begrudge the Disney Adults too much. Maudlin as they may be, nostalgia helps us tolerate the present in order to warm ourselves up to what's next. It's how we cope with what John Koenig called "avenoir," the impossible desire to see memories in advance. "We take it for granted that life moves forward. But you move as a rower moves, facing backwards: you can see where you've been, but not where you're going," Koenig wrote in *The Dictionary of Obscure Sorrows*. "Your boat is steered by a younger version of you. It's hard not to wonder what life would be like facing the other way."

Casey loves nostalgia. Because we grew up together, the feeling is always humming somewhere in the background of our relationship. Sometimes I'll hold my fork or scrunch my nose a certain way, and he'll burst out, "That's *so* high school Mandy." There's anemoia in Casey's music, too. I can hear it in his melodic contours, which even in high school had a dreamlike 1940s quality to them, layered with all the eclectic textures afforded by digital music-making, so every composition sounds like a song he knew in a past life, played on an instrument from the future. "Nostalgia is a powerful creative tool, because it sits at the border of real and imaginary. It lets you turn events from your own life into fantasies," Casey said. An Ella Fitzgerald song will come on his Spotify, and he'll cry out from the other room, "I was born in the wrong era!" Then the playlist will serve him a James Blake track, then Childish Gambino, John Mayer, Ariana Grande, Michael Bublé, and he'll reconsider: "Never mind!" Like that toadstool LED night light, there's magic in crossing visions of the past and future in a way that could only be possible right now.

Toward the end of each interview I conducted for this book, I posed my sources a personal question: If time travel were possible, was there any period other than the present they'd want to live in? Not a single therapist, historian, or behavioral economist answered yes.

"Even with all the challenges of now, I couldn't tell you another time I'd prefer," said Linda Sanderville, a D.C. therapist specializing in support for women of color. "I'm not someone who's like, oh look how wonderful everything is right now, but just look at dying in childbirth. That's still a major issue in the Black maternal community—I'm a mother of two little boys, so that's definitely important to me—and

2022 taught us just how shaky women's rights still are in general, but the past was *way* worse in almost every way."

"I know it's hard to believe," added language psychologist David Ludden, when we spoke in early 2022. "We've got a worldwide pandemic going on, and it doesn't seem like the best of times. But actually, it is. I mean, look, you're in Los Angeles and I'm on the other side of the country, and yet, here we are, talking about these ideas."

Last year, climate activist and author of *The Intersectional Environmentalist* Leah Thomas told me that there's been a shift in her field away from attitudes of pure dismantling and toward "radical imagination." In the past, she said, it was always easy for her to identify the oppressors she was fighting, but if someone were to ask about the future she was building, she couldn't answer with as much clarity. "And that made me sad," said Thomas. "So I've been spending more time thinking about [the] future and about joy because . . . joy is such a powerful motivator, when shame can never motivate you in the same way."

To tap into her most radically imaginative self, Sanderville frees up periodic slices of time not to consume any media at all. Not the internet, not television, not even books. "It's hard to consume and create in the same state," she told me. "If you value any kind of creativity, and I don't just mean art, give your brain a break from consuming, because that gives you space to process all that you've been reading or watching." We must afford ourselves this space actively, said Sanderville, because at life's current pace, it won't happen by accident. "Ask: How can you figure out a way to be grinding less so that you can be more creative, more influential? How can you spend your energy on the things that deeply matter to you?"

My all-time favorite nostalgic TV rewatch is the early-2000s HBO series *Six Feet Under*. During bouts of distress, I'll flick on an episode or two of the dramedy about a family-run funeral home, and it feels like an embrace from a macabre fairy godmother. Let's just say if there were a *Six Feet Under* theme park, I'd be an annual pass holder. I'd pile my family into the station wagon to spend every other weekend riding bumper hearses and slurping strawberry milkshakes out of upcycled embalming fluid bottles. Anyway, the show is probably most famous for its iconic series finale. Spoiler alert, but the family's father and eldest son have already died, when the twenty-two-year-old daughter, an aspiring photographer, decides to move to New York City to try her luck at a new life. Before leaving, she gathers her remaining family members on the porch to snap a final portrait for posterity, when her brother's ghost appears beside her and whispers, "You can't take a picture of this. It's already gone." I swear, every time I watch the finale, that line means something different to me.

I've been thinking it might be a comment on nostalgia for the present. We're still missing a term for that obscure sorrow—a plaintive longing for what's happening right now, a futile hope that it never ends. I think we need one. Maybe coming up with a word to describe that feeling will help us feel it more. I propose "tempusur," a portmanteau of the Latin *tempus*, meaning "time," and *susurrus*, meaning "whisper."

Tempusur /tɛmp'əzɚ/: *n*. An elusive nostalgia for the current moment, so precious in its ephemerality that the second you notice it, it's already slipped away.

ELEVEN

THE LIFE-CHANGING MAGIC OF BECOMING A MEDIOCRE CRAFTER
A note on the IKEA effect

A therapist in a large beaded necklace once told me over video chat that in order to yank your attention into the present, you're supposed to do things with your hands. "Watercolors, card tricks, any hands-on hobby," she said, her kind eyes squinting glitchily over Zoom. I winced at the suggestion, as a sentiment from my hometown hero John Waters leapt to mind: "The only insult I've ever received in my adult life was when someone asked me, 'Do you have a hobby?' A HOBBY?! DO I LOOK LIKE A FUCKING DABBLER?!" I wanted to sneer, but then I remembered: Nora Ephron loved to cook. Michelle Obama has her knitting. Greta Thunberg allegedly cross-stitches for relaxation between climate justice meetings with presidents. None of it is what they're known for, but it's what they love. What they do with their hands. "A hobby," I told the therapist. "I'll think on it."

Unfortunately, I believe I might be the single worst crafter of all time. Since childhood, my instincts as a painter, a French braider, a friendship bracelet maker have been practically non-existent. I recognize that a woman publicly admitting to her lack of domesticity is still taboo, or at least unflattering, like someone confessing they don't like dogs. For the record, I have made heartfelt attempts at "dabbling." During the craft boom of the 2020 lockdown, I managed to grow a small forest of basil, though I manslaughtered it within a matter of days. I tried pouring candles, but they reeked of funeral flowers. Upon burning one, I was blighted by a headache so enfeebling that I spent the rest of the afternoon supine in the dark with a peppermint lozenge. Casey wanted to help. He procured me a beginner's pottery kit, then a loom. Neither was assembled. Dismayed by my own incompetence, I became obsessed with a category of "homesteading influencers," young internet celebrities who seemed to possess every DIY skill that I didn't. I grew particularly infatuated with one figure named Isabel, who produced weekly films about her life off the grid in the verdant forests of Washington State. In her early twenties with russet hair to her waist, Isabel built her own house by hand wearing a sundress and work boots, cultivated and cooked her own vegan cornucopias, weaved throw blankets from yarn she spun herself, and traveled into town for WiFi access once a week to upload. The girl knew her way around a spinning wheel better than I knew mine around my own television remote. I was as enchanted by her as I was ashamed of myself. Crafting seemed to fulfill almost everyone else on earth but me. Why was I so incapable of this basic human joy?

Then, like falling in love after a lifetime of loneliness, I discovered the art of flipping furniture.

A little under a year into quarantine, my best friend Racheli and I stumbled across the practice online. Or really, it stumbled toward us, and we lunged back. Some crafts like embroidery and dollhouse-making are painstaking, but furniture-flipping is broad-stroked and flashy, the gratification instant. Perfect for an anxious dilettante. A brief tutorial: You start by purchasing used home goods—mirrors, lamps, accent chairs—for dirt cheap from yard sales and secondhand stores. You might even find viable candidates in the back of your closet. You form an eye for both neglect and potential. You gussy up your wares by slapping on a coat of paint or even just wiping the piece clean and staging it so it approximates something you'd find new for ten times the price. There are more advanced flipping techniques involving upholstery and power tools; assess your capabilities accordingly. Finally, do with the final product whatever you wish: Keep or sell. Give away to a friend.

Each Saturday, Racheli and I collected a batch of new tchotchkes, then descended upon the craft store, devoting our entire weekend to "restoring" in time to list the finished products on Facebook Marketplace Sunday night. The point was not to profit, and we almost never did, mostly breaking even but relishing the endeavor anyway like a catch-and-release fishing trip.

Of all our projects, my favorite flip began as a dusty seashell lamp the color of mucus. Racheli and I found it for $10 at a neighborhood Goodwill and decided to take a risk. Decor in the style of 1980s Miami was enjoying a wacky revival, so we seized the moment by painting the lamp a shade of atrocious Hubba-Bubba-Bubble-Tape pink. "This thing is fugly. I feel bad selling it," said Racheli. Before the flip, we'd mentally priced the lamp at $20, but the moment we placed our grubby little paws on it, some primal ghost took over. By the time the final pink paint coat dried, we concluded that with the right viral TikTok, the lamp could sell for hundreds. Let me reiterate, this object was grotesque. It looked like SpongeBob SquarePants's pet snail, Gary. Thirty minutes prior, we saw that plainly. Now, we were listing it on the internet for the average price of a bottle of Veuve Clicquot. For a moment, I thought I actually wanted to keep the lamp. For a moment, I thought I might leave my godless, city-slicked existence behind and move to the mountains to flip seashell lamps full-time. I'd wear tasseled kaftans and dwell in a yurt that doubled as my craft studio. I'd macramé shawls. I'd throw pottery. I'd keep goats. Finally, I'd master the loom. I'd invite influencer Isabel to come live with me and spend the next decade as her apprentice. For a moment, that seashell lamp illuminated a vision for my pastoral future. Hope swelled within me like a ripe peach.

Our lamp sold above asking price to a shiny-haired college student within an hour of posting. But it was never about the money. It was about that feeling. Finally, I grasped what that therapist meant. Nothing satisfies the spirit quite like building something yourself, or at least helping to. At the same time, nothing had ever warped my perception of "value" with such efficiency. What is it about a human hand?

The propensity to ascribe disproportionately high worth to items we helped create is a cognitive bias, known as the *IKEA effect*. Its delightful name is an homage to the Swedish furniture company whose affordable products require assembly. Spending long nights splayed on the floor, struggling to piece together IKEA Malm chests and POÄNG chairs, is practically a coming-of-age ritual, a contemporary rite of passage as significant as the Amish Rumspringa. Erect your first anticlimactic IKEA dresser, and you finally know what it means to stitch a tiny fabric square to the quilt of humanity.

The IKEA effect was first documented in 2011, when a trio of Ivy League researchers demonstrated the intrinsic urge for people to bloat the valuation of products they helped construct. The experiment, led by Harvard behavioral scientist Michael I. Norton, invited consumers to build Lego sets, fold origami, and assemble IKEA boxes. Even if the participants expressed zero interest or enjoyment in DIY hobbies—and even if the results of their efforts were as shoddy as Racheli's and my seashell lamp—as long as they saw their projects to completion, they swelled with satisfaction. The research subjects expressed willingness to pay more for the products they built than they would for objectively superior versions that arrived pre-assembled. "Participants saw their amateurish creations ... as similar in value to the creations of experts, and expected others to share their opinions," concluded the authors. Thanks to my days as a mediocre furniture flipper, perusing this study felt like looking in a funhouse mirror.

The IKEA effect was observed long before it was described. An oft-cited example comes from the mid-twentieth century, during the golden age of processed food. As the anecdote goes, in 1947, General Mills launched a new line of Betty Crocker instant cake mixes that tasted nearly indistinguishable from the stuff made from scratch. The product took off at first, but sales eventually slowed to a near halt. In a state of consternation, General Mills solicited the analysis of a Freudian psychologist, who determined that this sales decline was a result of guilt. Homemakers felt that if all they did was add water, the cake was not truly *theirs*. They couldn't proudly tell their husbands and children that they'd prepared the fluffy confection with their own two hands. General Mills responded with an unexpected marketing pivot. They relaunched the instant cake mixes with a new slogan, "Add an Egg." Now, baking was easy but not *too* easy. Betty Crocker's sales soared.

The details of this eggy legend are up for debate (for one, adding fresh eggs isn't just a marketing ploy—it really does improve the taste of instant cake); but, its takeaway message stands: We like things better when we've had a hand in creating them. According to the IKEA effect's coiners, this fact isn't due merely to guilt, but rather something more existential. What truly displeased Betty Crocker consumers, they argued, was the sobering shock of insignificance. New technology insinuated that mothers' home cooking, and thus mothers themselves, were unnecessary. No one likes "the feeling of being rendered . . . irrelevant," commented Norton et al. The cake mix did not technically require additional ingredients, labor, or expertise, but that egg fulfilled consumers' desire for "effectance," the spiritually satisfying notion that we caused something to happen in the world. The egg made people feel like they mattered.

Since the 1950s, daily life has only become more automated, but the innate yearning for physical handprints has not disappeared. In theory, the IKEA effect is responsible for the entire DIY renaissance. The term "do-it-yourself" first bubbled up in consumer discourse in the early 1910s, but throughout mid-century America, as baking your own bread and renovating your own basement became not just economical practicalities but creative diversions, the phrase entered everyday conversation. By the 1970s, the coolly abbreviated "DIY" subculture gave rise to self-published books and zines, mixtape trading, "reduce, reuse, and recycle" practices inspired by the burgeoning environmental movement, and endless crocheted handicrafts.

With the launch of Pinterest in 2010, DIY took on major significance. Domestic "hacks" boomed from a casual hobby to a bona fide lifestyle. Since the early aughts, companies have capitalized on the IKEA effect, no longer treating customers as mere receivers of value but partners in its creation. Think of the colossal meal kit market: Subscription DIY-dinner companies like Blue Apron and Home Chef hypnotize busy professionals who don't have time to cook into proudly chopping, sautéeing, and braising a new recipe each night for nearly the same price as takeout (though not at all the same feeling). There's also the crowdfunding industry. Sites like Kickstarter and GoFundMe have lost millions of mini-"investor" dollars due to failed and never-launched products, but the hope of helping to birth a new video game or nano drone is still so arousing that the industry has soared to over $20 billion. One could argue that the IKEA effect is the whole driving force behind TikTok's popularity. The platform's interactive atmosphere—including its "stitch" feature and hyper-engaged comments sections—encourages audiences to become co-creators, producers, and critics. Mainstream artists, too, have increasingly allowed patrons to shape their output. In 2018, at the urging of a Twitter fan, the band Weezer released a cover of Toto's "Africa," which became their first *Billboard* #1 hit single in ten years. It inspired an entire smash-hit covers album that practically relaunched the group's career. The album received mixed reviews from critics, but the magic was not in the music—it was in the co-creation.

The world is growing more user-generated. This is not necessarily because artists and entrepreneurs are out of ideas; it's because they recognize that brands are "communities" now, and if consumers don't feel seen and held by their communities, they won't feel important. They won't come back. To feel like we're contributing to the world, lending a hand at cultivating our vegetable medleys and video games, is searingly important. We need the allegorical egg. The egg gives us purpose. The egg tells us we deserve to be here. But what happens when the egg becomes so obsolete that we can't even pretend to need it anymore?

In 2020, a sound bite exploded on TikTok that went, "Darling, I have no dream job. I do not dream of labor."* The moment was one of widespread ennui. The term "languishing" had taken off in a *New York Times* piece by Adam Grant, assigning a validating label to a chronic cultural plague. We were failing to make progress, so people decided to critique the value of progress in the first place. A whole category of viral memes spun off the original. Among my favorites read, "I do not want to be a woman in the work force!!! I want to be a little creature drinking from a creek!!!!!!"

Indeed, conflating self-worth with employment is one of capitalism's wiliest tricks, but research finds that both humans and little creatures by creeks do appreciate (if not

---

* The quote's origins are unverified. Shocking for TikTok, I know!

dream about) a certain amount of labor. In a 2009 survey, responders rated their jobs among their least pleasurable daily activities, but also their most rewarding. That might sound like toxic productivity brainwashing, but a similar intuition exists in nonhumans—even rats and starlings prefer food sources that require exertion to obtain. Some jobs are inherently more satisfying than others: A 2023 analysis of American time use from the Bureau of Labor Statistics concluded that out of all career pursuits, the highest levels of happiness were reported by loggers, a line of work involving both labor by hand and the curative outdoors. (The most stressful, least gratifying occupations were finance, insurance, and most of all, law.) Jobs that either don't click with some natural facet of the human spirit, or don't produce a livable income, are about as "rewarding" as a lab rat toiling through a gray-walled maze, only to receive half a crumb.

Like the sunk cost fallacy, the IKEA effect is at its core another effort justification bias. How we love to defend our most expensive, time-consuming, irreversible choices. The ironic link between a task's arduousness or permanence and our eagerness to rationalize it is why, when faced with a heavy decision—like whether or not to attend grad school or have another kid—psychologists caution against asking the advice of someone who just did it themselves. If a person endures involuntary pain on their path toward achievement (say, if they get a paper cut while folding origami, or are forced to finish out a prison sentence), that won't make them appreciate the end result any more. But if they *willingly* endure suffering (if they opt to get the paper cut, or throw a wedding the price of a down payment), that paper crane will start to look like it's made of porcelain.

The IKEA effect isn't all outright fantasy. The social connection it fosters is real, especially when the end product is tangible. As much as automation and specialization have benefited society, they risk limiting our social engagement. DIY projects offer the chance for more holistic, communal modes of interaction. Furniture-flipping with Racheli was pure jubilance even though we were bad at it, because we did it together. Adorably, the Norton study found that after completing their origami and Lego structures, participants expressed a desire to show them to their friends. It doesn't take a psychologist to intuit that sharing an object you made inspires much more pleasure than displaying something you bought or something that technically belongs to a large company. This is even and especially true when the creation didn't turn out quite as planned.

As a thirtieth birthday present to myself, I procured my first ever work-from-home desk and chair (from Facebook Marketplace, obviously). The chair, chosen for its sleek beechwood-and-steel swivel, was not particularly cozy for the derriere, but feeling high on my new rig and emboldened by my furniture-flipping stint, I decided to try and DIY myself a seat cushion. I purchased a needle, thread, and a yard of faux suede fabric in a peacock-green shade. Then, repurposing the innards of a neglected dog toy, I sutured a pillow the size and shape of a personal pizza. This seat cushion is the most unremarkable object in my home. I believe it is a masterpiece. The seat cushion is every instant Funfetti cake on earth. It is my Sistine Chapel. I show it to everyone. When friends and family come to visit, I lead them to my dainty home office as if about to unveil a sculpture chiseled from marble, and when I gleefully lift the wilted disc from my chair, they smile at me the way one who doesn't care for children humors their little niece's living room "play." I see this happen. I do not care. I am prouder of my seat cushion than I am of this book. I was practically foaming at the mouth to tell you about it. I am sitting on it *right now*.*

Seat cushions and seashell lamps aren't the world's costliest objects, but the IKEA effect also holds for higher price brackets. The Norton study noted homeowners' pride in their tawdry home improvements—lopsidedly laid walkways, sloppily constructed firepits—believing they'll make the house more attractive to friends and prospective buyers, even when they do just the opposite. I go window-shopping for overpriced homes on Zillow almost every day and have seen some kitschy personalizations: self-assembled tiki bars, an amateur pizza oven shaped like a hippopotamus. I feel for the realtors who chose not to inform the owners that those

---

* Needles and fabric do wonders for the spirit. A study published in the *British Journal of Occupational Therapy* surveyed over 3,500 knitters and found that 81 percent of participants with depression reported feeling happy post-knitting. More than 50 percent said they felt "very happy."

quirks weren't quite the assets they thought they were. (My seat cushion absolutely is, though.) These imperfections may not be optimized for profit, but they are what make us wince and laugh and spark conversation. Flaws are what give a thing life.

One day fairly soon, some argue that AI-generated art will surpass humans' abilities so greatly that no egg could ever make up for our impertinence. In 2018, one of the first AI paintings to be sold at auction went for $432,500. On the bottom right of the canvas, its signature read *min G max D x [log (D(x))] + z [log (1 -D (G(z)))]*, part of the code that produced it. Titled *Edmond de Belamy*, the image depicts a portly French gentleman in a black coat and white collar—the painting style frenetic, distorted, *almost* nineteenth-century Impressionist but some quality just askew. Cock your head to the right, and the portrait narrowly resembles "Monkey Christ," a botched restoration of a 1930s Christian fresco that turned out so ludicrously simian, it went viral in the late 2010s, attracting a wryly worshipful cult following. Tourists now flock to the small town in Spain where "Monkey Christ" is displayed, just to bask in its blundered glory.

It's hard to imagine humans rallying around an AI portrait with "Monkey Christ"–level verve. *Edmond de Belamy* might have been worth half a million dollars to a Beverly Hills art collector, but I remain unconvinced that a robot-generated art piece could emit the je ne sais quoi necessary to lure pilgrims. For all its sophistication, a machine can't guffaw at the absurdity of sewing a bad seat cushion and then showing it off to its friends. That kind of effrontery is an inside joke shared by humans alone.

In 2019, a fan of the Australian musician Nick Cave wrote in to his blog and asked, "Considering human imagination the last piece of wilderness, do you think A.I. will ever be able to write a good song?" "Good" meaning more than technically impressive. Cave was dubious. "What a great song makes us feel is a sense of awe," he responded. There's that notion of awe again; Cave characterized it as being "almost exclusively predicated on our limitations. . . . It is entirely to do with our audacity as humans to reach beyond our potential." By Cave's measure, as impressive as posthuman creativity might be, it "simply doesn't have this capacity. How could it?"

How could it? The question haunted me. One morning in early 2023, Casey and I found ourselves puzzling through the answer as we drove home from our favorite coffee shop in L.A., whose iced cortados are a thing of immeasurable beauty. Casey is a film composer, so the creation of music is of both material and existential concern to him. Heading east, as a talon of marigold sunlight pierced through our windshield, we rummaged for reasons why a machine could never replicate the soulfulness of human touch, only to realize with sorrow that perhaps those reasons don't exist. It's no stretch to picture AI figuring out how to approximate the texture of our audacity, or invent its very own, well enough to inspire awe. As Casey and I pulled into the driveway, a film of melancholy draped over us like a top sheet. "It just makes everything I do feel so small," he exhaled.

Lingering in park, Casey thumbed his coffee condensation. For us, this type of digital-age nihilism is inevitable, but we treat it like a heavy water jug. When one of us gets too tired to carry it, the other takes a turn. Then, it becomes the job of the unburdened partner to distract the other, reminding them that life can feel weightless, too. So I told Casey that a robot could compose the most enchanting concerto of all time, and it would never be as valuable to me as the nightly waltzes he improvises on our upright Wurlitzer for the sheer fact that he's the one making them. It feels good to paint an old seashell lamp alone. It feels better to have a doting witness.

Placing us in competition with technology might not even be the most functional line of questioning to pursue anyway. In 2014, the singer Claire L. Evans called our judgments of AI's ability to "pass" as human musicians "almost exquisitely myopic." Our cars do not "pass" as horses, but they do an excellent job carting us around. PowerThesaurus.com does not "pass" as my brain, but I happily used it while writing this book. Combine hyper-advanced technology with humans' visceral inventiveness, and you get sorcery. The best instant cake mix in the world can't pipe a ridiculous inside joke in glow-in-the-dark icing on top, but with all that time you saved not baking the thing, you can have your cake, and well, you know the rest.

The winter that I began my second draft of this book, I was stuck home alone for a week with COVID and decided to pass the time testing the emotional limits of ChatGPT. In our most notable exchange, I asked the chatbot what it believed to be humans' versus AI's single greatest strengths. It responded that AI's best asset is reason, while humans' is love. I found the answer poignant, though I'm not convinced it's true. Who says we have to choose?

Perhaps we will always feel like we're on the outermost brink of losing touch with our primal selves, like any second now, the egg could disappear around the corner forever. Perhaps we should get used to existing in that state. I suspect we've already been there for a long time. In 1962, Sylvia Plath suggested a critique of the exceptionalist attitude that society had, just then, reached an unprecedented point of inhumanity. In a short essay titled "Context," Plath problematized what she called "headline poetry"—choosing to reference the era's major political conflicts (Hiroshima, the Cold War) so directly and sensationally in poems, as if the mid-twentieth century was sure to go down as the most worrying time in history and should be immortalized as such. Plath challenged readers to widen their lens. "For me," she contended, "the real issues of our time are the issues of every time—the hurt and wonder of loving; making in all its forms—children, loaves of bread, paintings, buildings; and the conservation of life of all people in all places, the jeopardizing of which no abstract doubletalk of 'peace' or 'implacable foes' can excuse." It is perhaps no coincidence that Plath wrote this essay the same year she began keeping bees, a craft that inspired many of her most iconic poems. Love, survival, creation by hand. Technology changes faster than the lifespan of a honeybee, but we are the hive.

Acknowledgments

Thank you to my editor, Julia Cheiffetz. I can't tell you what your dedication and belief in me has meant. Thank you for splaying across the floor of your office with me, pushing me to rise to the occasion of this book, and dotting my wrists with peppermint oil when it all got to be too much. I feel unfathomably lucky to have had both your keen eye and confidence. I am the honeybee; you are the hive.

Thank you as always to Rachel Vogel, the best literary agent in the world. You are the moon to my manifestation circle, the UFO to my alien. Thanks to you, I have not completely lost my mind.

Thank you to Abby Mohr for the careful reads and meticulous note-taking. To Haley Hamilton for the invaluable research assistance. To James Iacobelli and Laywan Kwan for the smash of a cover.

ACKNOWLEDGMENTS

Thank you to my brilliant friends, especially the ones whose brains I mined for this book: Koa Beck, Tori Hill, Amanda Kohr, Sheila Marikar, Adison Marshall, Coco Mellors, Kristin Mortensen, Racheli Peltier, Will Plunkett, Rachel Torres, and Alisson Wood. My gratitude as well to Olivia Blaustein, Nicholas Ciani, Katie Epperson, Morgan Hoit, Carly Hugo, Ally McGivney, Nora McInerny, Jordan Moore, Matt Parker, Jacy Schleier, Ashley Silver, and Drew Welborn.

Thank you to the lovely readers who've connected with me online over the years. Even on the uncanny plane of Instagram, I can feel your enthusiasm and encouragement, and I am so appreciative.

Thank you to the brilliant scholars who generously shared their expertise with me for this project, especially Minaa B., Dena DiNardo, Ramani Durvasula, Eleanor Janega, Sekoul Krastev, David Ludden, Frank McAndrew, Moiya McTier, Tom Mould, and Linda Sanderville.

Thank you to my nonhuman assistants, my beloved feline and canine children Claire, Fiddle, and Teddy Roo. And to my dearly departed angels David and Arthur Moon, who were both made of pure magic.

Thank you to my mom Denise, dad Craig, and brother Brandon for instilling in me the best possible blend of logos and pathos. Thank you for letting me include you as characters

ACKNOWLEDGMENTS

in my work, even though it's impossible to do you justice. I am in dinosaur-level awe of you, always.

Thank you to the love of my life, Casey Kolb, the composer of my life's soundtrack and forever protagonist. I wrote this book for you. If you don't love it, please just lie like the husband in the Julia Louis-Dreyfus movie.

This is the book I've always dreamt of writing. Pardon the dramatics, but the fact that I got to do it makes me feel like I can die happy. Thank you all for reading.

NOTES

Make It Make Sense

2 *the nation's mental health:* Edmund S. Higgins, "Is Mental Health Declining in the U.S.?," *Scientific American*, January 1, 2017. https://www.scientificamerican.com/article/is-mental-health-declining-in-the-u-s/.

2 *a CDC survey:* "Youth Risk Behavior Survey Data Summary & Trends Report: 2011–2021," Centers for Disease Control and Prevention. Accessed September 21, 2023. https://www.cdc.gov/healthyyouth/data/yrbs/index.htm.

2 *crisis calls to their lifeline:* "Coming 'Together for Mental Health' Is NAMI's Urgent Appeal During May's Mental Health Awareness Month," NAMI, May 2, 2022. https://www.nami.org/Press-Media/Press-Releases/2022/Coming-Together-for-Mental-Health%E2%80%9D-Is-NAMI-s-Urgent-Appeal-During-May-s-Mental-Health-Awareness-Mon#:~:text=Between%202020%20and%202021%2C%20calls,health%20crises%20increased%20by%2051%25.

3 *Marxist philosopher Frantz Fanon:* Edmund Burke, "Frantz Fanon's 'The Wretched of the Earth,'" *Daedalus* 105, no. 1 (1976): 127–35. http://www.jstor.org/stable/20024388.

3 *coined in 1972 by behavioral economists:* Georg Bruckmaier, Stefan Krauss, Karin Binder, Sven Hilbert, and Martin Brunner, "Tversky and Kahneman's Cognitive Illusions: Who Can Solve Them, and Why?," *Frontiers in Psychology* 12 (April 12, 2021). https://doi.org/10.3389/fpsyg.2021.584689.

5 *said Jessica Grose:* "Jess Grose." X—Formerly Twitter. Accessed September 21, 2023. https://twitter.com/JessGrose.

6 *"The most basic activism":* Kevin Powell and bell hooks, "The BK Nation Interview with bell hooks," *Other*, February 28, 2014. https://web.archive.org/web/20140624015000/https://bknation.org/2014/02/bk-nation-interview-bell-hooks/.

NOTES

1. Are You My Mother, Taylor Swift?

15 *a Japanese study:* Miharu Nakanish et al., "The Association Between Role Model Presence and Self-Regulation in Early Adolescence: A Cross-Sectional Study," *PLOS One* 14, no. 9 (September 19, 2019). https://doi.org/10.1371/journal.pone.0222752.

15 *A 2021 study:* Lynn McCutcheon and Mara S. Aruguete, "Is Celebrity Worship Increasing Over Time?," *Journal of Social Sciences and Humanities* 7, no. 1 (April 2021): 66–75.

16 *In a* New York Times *op-ed:* "When Did We Start Taking Famous People Seriously?," *New York Times*, April 20, 2020. https://www.nytimes.com/2020/04/20/parenting/celebrity-activism-politics.html.

16 *three quarters of Americans:* "Public Trust in Government: 1958–2022," Pew Research Center, June 6, 2022. https://www.pewresearch.org/politics/2022/06/06/public-trust-in-government-1958-2022/.

18 *analyzed NPR music reporter Sidney Madden:* Sidney Madden, Stephen Thompson, Ann Powers, and Joshua Bote, "The 2010s: Social Media and the Birth of Stan Culture," NPR, October 17, 2019. https://www.npr.org/2019/10/07/767903704/the-2010s-social-media-and-the-birth-of-stan-culture.

18 *"Tumblr opened my eyes":* Danielle Colin-Thome, "Fan Culture Can Be Wildly Empowering—And At Times, Wildly Problematic," *Bustle*, July 24, 2018. https://www.bustle.com/p/fan-culture-can-be-wildly-empowering-at-times-wildly-problematic-9836745.

18 *A 2014 clinical examination:* Randy A. Sansone and Lori A. Sansone, "'I'm Your Number One Fan'—A Clinical Look at Celebrity Worship," *Innovations in Clinical Neuroscience* 11, no. 1–2 (2014): 39–43.

19 *This 2005 study:* Lorraine Sheridan, Adrian C. North, John Maltby, and Raphael Gillett, "Celebrity Worship, Addiction and Criminality," *Psychology, Crime & Law* 13, no. 6 (2007): 559–71. https://doi.org/10.1080/10683160601160653.

20 *said Jill Gutowitz:* "The Cult of Taylor Swift," *Sounds Like a Cult*, October 18, 2022. https://open.spotify.com/episode/5yMUPSoX46ArUPYJNNx4nm.

20 *a humorous review:* Jill Gutowitz, "What Is Every Song on Taylor Swift's Lover Actually About?," *Vulture*, August 23, 2019. https://www.vulture.com/2019/08/taylor-swifts-lover-album-meaning-and-analysis.html.

NOTES

22 *One study from the mid-2000s:* Lynn McCutcheon, "Exploring the link between attachment and the inclination to obsess about or stalk celebrities," *North American Journal of Psychology*, June 2006, https://www.researchgate.net/publication/286333358_Exploring_the_link_between_attachment_and_the_inclination_to_obsess_about_or_stalk_celebrities.

22 *a pair of studies:* Ágnes Zsila and Zsolt Demetrovics, "Psychology of celebrity worship: A literature review," *Psychiatria Hungarica*, 2020, https://pubmed.ncbi.nlm.nih.gov/32643621/.

22 *"positive stressors":* Yiqing He and Ying Sun, "Breaking up with my idol: A qualitative study of the psychological adaptation process of renouncing fanship," *Frontiers in Psychology*, December, 16, 2022, https://www.ncbi.nlm.nih.gov/pmc/articles/PMC9803266/.

22 *a similar survey out of Hong Kong:* Chau-kiu Cheung and Xiao Dong Yue, "Idol Worship as Compensation for Parental Absence," *International Journal of Adolescence and Youth* 17, no. 1 (2012): 35–46. https://doi.org/10.1080/02673843.2011.649399.

22 *said psychotherapist Mark Epstein:* Mark Epstein, *The Trauma of Everyday Life* (New York: Penguin, 2014).

23 *her analysis of the bash:* Amanda Petrusich, "The Startling Intimacy of Taylor Swift's Eras Tour," *The New Yorker*, June 12, 2023. https://www.newyorker.com/magazine/2023/06/19/taylor-swift-eras-tour-review.

24 *a survey of 833 Chinese teenagers:* Chau-kiu Cheung and Xiao Dong Yue, "Identity Achievement and Idol Worship Among Teenagers in Hong Kong," *International Journal of Adolescence and Youth* 11, no. 1 (2003): 1–26. https://doi.org/10.1080/02673843.2003.9747914.

25 *Canadian political columnist Sabrina Maddeaux:* Sabrina Maddeaux, "How the Urge to Dehumanize Celebrities Takes a Dark Turn When They Become Victims—Not Just of Lip Injections," *National Post*, October 11, 2016. https://nationalpost.com/entertainment/celebrity/how-the-urge-to-dehumanize-celebrities-takes-a-dark-turn-when-they-become-victims-not-just-of-lip-injections.

25 *ventriloquized women's voices:* Jared Richards, "Charli XCX's Queer Male Fans Need to Do Better," *Junkee*, October 30, 2019. https://junkee.com/charli-xcx-poppers-douche-queer-gay-fans/226620.

26 *In 1953, English pediatrician and psychoanalyst Donald Winnicott:* D. W. Winnicott, *The Child, the Family, and the Outside World* (New York: Penguin, 1973), p. 173.

NOTES

27 *said Dr. Carla Naumburg:* Carla Naumburg, "The Gift of the Good Enough Mother," *Seleni*. Accessed September 21, 2023. https://www.seleni.org/advice-support/2018/3/14/the-gift-of-the-good-enough-mother.

27 *"The Year of the Cannibal":* Brenna Ehrlich, "2022 Was the Year of the Cannibal. What Does That Say About Us?," *Rolling Stone*, December 28, 2022. https://www.rollingstone.com/tv-movies/tv-movie-features/cannibal-2022-dahmer-yellowjackets-fresh-bones-and-all-timothee-chalamet-tv-movies-1234647553/.

2. I Swear I Manifested This

32 *58 percent of adults:* Giancarlo Pasquini and Scott Keeter, "At Least Four-in-Ten U.S. Adults Have Faced High Levels of Psychological Distress During COVID-19 Pandemic," Pew Research Center, December 12, 2022. https://www.pewresearch.org/short-reads/2022/12/12/at-least-four-in-ten-u-s-adults-have-faced-high-levels-of-psychological-distress-during-covid-19-pandemic/.

32 The New York Times *reported that teenagers:* Christina Caron. "Teens Turn to TikTok in Search of a Mental Health Diagnosis," *New York Times*, October 29, 2022. https://www.nytimes.com/2022/10/29/well/mind/tiktok-mental-illness-diagnosis.html.

33 *20 percent of Americans:* Katherine Schaeffer, "A Look at the Americans Who Believe There Is Some Truth to the Conspiracy Theory That COVID-19 Was Planned," Pew Research Center, July 24, 2020. https://www.pewresearch.org/short-reads/2020/07/24/a-look-at-the-americans-who-believe-there-is-some-truth-to-the-conspiracy-theory-that-covid-19-was-planned/.

33 *17 percent of respondents believed:* Marisa Meltzer, "QAnon's Unexpected Roots in New Age Spirituality," *Washington Post*, March 29, 2021. https://www.washingtonpost.com/magazine/2021/03/29/qanon-new-age-spirituality/.

35 *a British review:* Karen M. Douglas, Robbie M. Sutton, and Aleksandra Cichocka, "Belief in Conspiracy Theories: Looking Beyond Gullibility," *The Social Psychology of Gullibility*, April 2019, 61–76. https://doi.org/10.4324/9780429203787-4.

37 *"therapeutic but not therapy":* Sangeeta Singh-Kurtz, "I Tried Peoplehood, 'a Workout for Your Relationships'," *The Cut*, April 25, 2023. https://www.thecut.com/article/peoplehood-soulcycle.html

40 *"spiritual bypassing":* Rose Truesdale, "The Manifestation Business Moves Past Positive Thinking and Into Science," *Vice*, April 20, 2021.

NOTES

https://www.vice.com/en/article/3aq8ej/to-be-magnetic-manifestation-business-moves-past-positive-thinking-and-into-science.

41 *"Disinformation Dozen":* Shannon Bond, "Just 12 People Are Behind Most Vaccine Hoaxes on Social Media, Research Shows," NPR, May 14, 2021. https://www.npr.org/2021/05/13/996570855/disinformation-dozen-test-facebooks-twitters-ability-to-curb-vaccine-hoaxes.

42 *a $211,000 FTC fine:* "FTC Takes Action Against Lions Not Sheep and Owner for Slapping Bogus Made in USA Labels on Clothing Imported from China," Federal Trade Commission, May 11, 2022. https://www.ftc.gov/news-events/news/press-releases/2022/05/ftc-takes-action-against-lions-not-sheep-owner-slapping-bogus-made-usa-labels-clothing-imported.

44 *true stories take six times longer:* Peter Dizikes, "Study: On Twitter, False News Travels Faster Than True Stories," MIT News, Massachusetts Institute of Technology, March 8, 2018. https://news.mit.edu/2018/study-twitter-false-news-travels-faster-true-stories-0308.

44 *said Sinan Aral:* Maggie Fox, "Fake News: Lies Spread Faster on Social Media Than Truth Does," NBCNews.com, March 9, 2018. https://www.nbcnews.com/health/health-news/fake-news-lies-spread-faster-social-media-truth-does-n854896.

45 *"no advertising rule":* Farah Naz Khan, "Beware of Social Media Celebrity Doctors," Scientific American Blog Network, September 6, 2017. https://blogs.scientificamerican.com/observations/beware-of-social-media-celebrity-doctors/.

50 *How's this for a healthcare conspiracy:* Ann Pietrangelo, "What the Baader-Meinhof Phenomenon Is and Why You May See It Again . . . and Again," *Healthline*, December 17, 2019. https://www.healthline.com/health/baader-meinhof-phenomenon.

51 In his book *The Myth of Normal:* Gabor Maté, *The Myth of Normal* (London: Random House UK, 2023).

3. A Toxic Relationship Is Just a Cult of One

52 *"To love someone is":* Rebecca Solnit, *The Faraway Nearby* (New York: Viking, 2013).

52 *sunk cost fallacy:* "Why Are We Likely to Continue with an Investment Even if It Would Be Rational to Give It Up?," The Decision Lab. Accessed August 21, 2023. https://thedecisionlab.com/biases/the-sunk-cost-fallacy.

NOTES

53 *Didion said:* Joan Didion, *The Year of Magical Thinking* (New York: Random House Large Print, 2008).

59 *a Brown University philosophy professor:* Ryan Doody, "The Sunk Cost 'Fallacy' Is Not a Fallacy," *Ergo, an Open Access Journal of Philosophy*, 2019. https://quod.lib.umich.edu/e/ergo/12405314.0006.040/--sunk-cost-fallacy-is-not-a-fallacy?rgn=main%3Bview.

60 *amygdalas make snap conclusions:* Alexandra Sifferlin, "Our Brains Immediately Judge People," *Time*, August 6, 2014. https://time.com/3083667/brain-trustworthiness/.

63 *adding or removing colored blocks:* Benjamin A. Converse, Gabrielle S. Adams, Andrew H. Hales, and Leidy E. Klotz, "We Instinctively Add on New Features and Fixes. Why Don't We Subtract Instead?," Frank Batten School of Leadership and Public Policy, University of Virginia, April 16, 2021. https://batten.virginia.edu/about/news/we-instinctively-add-new-features-and-fixes-why-dont-we-subtract-instead.

66 *experiencing emotional abuse:* Adam Nesenoff, "What Is Emotional Abuse?," Tikvah Lake, July 7, 2020. https://www.tikvahlake.com/blog/what-is-emotional-abuse/#:~:text=Although%20difficult%20to%20measure%2C%20research,affects%2011%20percent%20of%20children.

4. The Shit-Talking Hypothesis

70 *"Beauty is terror":* Donna Tartt, *The Secret History* (New York: Alfred A. Knopf, 1992).

71 *"lipstick effect":* Eve Pearl, "The Lipstick Effect of 2009," *HuffPost*, November 17, 2011. https://www.huffpost.com/entry/the-lipstick-effect-of-20_b_175533#:~:text=History%20and%20research%20has%20shown,years%20from%201929%20to%201933.

72 *Famously preoccupied by aesthetics:* Emily Van Duyne, "Sylvia Plath Looked Good in a Bikini—Deal With It," *Electric Literature*, October 9, 2017. https://electricliterature.com/sylvia-plath-looked-good-in-a-bikini-deal-with-it/.

73 *"Bell Jar":* The Bangles, "Bell Jar," Sony BMG Music Management, 1988. Accessed August 23, 1988. https://open.spotify.com/track/6ermpvXoKsD7NVGfVoap6u?si=2b96d03bffa7457d.

74 *zero-sum bias:* Daniel V. Meegan, "Zero-Sum Bias: Perceived Competition Despite Unlimited Resources," *Frontiers in Psychology*, November 2010. https://www.frontiersin.org/articles/10.3389/fpsyg.2010.00191

/full#:~:text=Zero%2Dsum%20bias%20describes%20intuitively,actually%20non%2Dzero%2Dsum.

74 *mistaken judgment:* Joseph Sunde, "'Win-Win Denial': The Roots of Zero-Sum Thinking," Acton Institute, September 14, 2021. https://rlo.acton.org/archives/122444-win-win-denial-the-roots-of-zero-sum-thinking.html.

74 *everyday misbeliefs:* Samuel G. B. Johnson, Jiewen Zhang, and Frank C Keil, "Win–Win Denial: The Psychological Underpinnings of Zero-Sum Thinking," American Psychological Association, 2022. https://psycnet.apa.org/record/2021-73979-001.

75 *"folk economics":* Pascal Boyer and Michael Bang Petersen, "Folk-Economic Beliefs: An Evolutionary Cognitive Model," *Behavioral and Brain Sciences* 41 (2018): e158. doi:10.1017/S0140525X17001960.

77 *individualist societies:* Markus Kemmelmeier and Daphna Oyserman, "Gendered Influence of Downward Social Comparisons on Current and Possible Selves," *Journal of Social Issues* 57, no. 1 (2001): 129–48. https://doi.org/10.1111/0022-4537.00205.

78 *In 2017, a sequence of experiments:* Kari Paul, "Here's Why Most Americans Prefer to Be a 'Big Fish in a Small Pond,'" LSA, June 22, 2017. https://lsa.umich.edu/psych/news-events/all-news/graduate-news/here_s-why-most-americans-prefer-to-be-a-big-fish-in-a-small-pon.html.

78 *anti-trade policies:* David Nakamura and David Weigel, "Trump's Anti-Trade Rhetoric Rattles the Campaign Message of Clinton and Unions," *Washington Post*, July 4, 2016. https://www.washingtonpost.com/politics/trumps-anti-trade-rhetoric-rattles-the-campaign-message-of-clinton-and-unions/2016/07/04/45916d5c-3f92-11e6-a66f-aa6c1883b6b1_story.html.

81 *by elementary school:* Marjorie Valls, "Gender Differences in Social Comparison Processes and Self-Concept Among Students," *Frontiers in Education* 6 (January 11, 2022). https://www.frontiersin.org/articles/10.3389/feduc.2021.815619/full.

81 *A 2022 study:* Valls, "Gender Differences in Social Comparison Processes and Self-Concept Among Students."

81 *TikTok use disorder:* Peng Sha and Xiaoyu Dong, "Research on Adolescents Regarding the Indirect Effect of Depression, Anxiety, and Stress Between TikTok Use Disorder and Memory Loss," MDPI, August 21, 2021. https://www.mdpi.com/1660-4601/18/16/8820.

NOTES

82 *tokenizing marginalized individuals:* Jacob Tobia, *Sissy: A Coming-of-Gender Story* (Lewes, UK: GMC, 2019).

83 *psychological effects of venting:* Douglas A. Gentile, "Catharsis and Media Violence: A Conceptual Analysis," MDPI, December 13, 2013. https://www.mdpi.com/2075-4698/3/4/491.

87 *teens' constant internet usage:* Jonathan Haidt, "Get Phones Out of Schools Now," *The Atlantic*, June 6, 2023. https://www.theatlantic.com/ideas/archive/2023/06/ban-smartphones-phone-free-schools-social-media/674304/.

87 *wrote former U.S. surgeon general:* V.H. Murthy, *Together: The Healing Power of Human Connection in a Sometimes Lonely World.* (New York: Harper Wave, 2020).

88 *"Shine Theory":* Ann Friedman, "Shine Theory: Why Powerful Women Make the Greatest Friends," *The Cut*, May 31, 2013. https://www.thecut.com/2013/05/shine-theory-how-to-stop-female-competition.html.

5. What It's Like to Die Online

90 *survivorship bias:* "Why Do We Misjudge Groups by Only Looking at Specific Group Members?," The Decision Lab. Accessed August 28, 2023. https://thedecisionlab.com/biases/survivorship-bias.

90 *an article for* Marie Claire *magazine:* Amanda Montell, "What It's Like to Die Online," *Marie Claire*, March 13, 2018. https://www.marieclaire.com/culture/a19183515/chronically-ill-youtube-stars/.

96 *fighter planes:* Jonathan Jarry, "Tips for Better Thinking: Surviving Is Only Half the Story," Office for Science and Society, October 6, 2020. https://www.mcgill.ca/oss/article/general-science/tips-better-thinking-surviving-only-half-story.

100 *less likely to have their medical needs met:* Elham Mahmoudi and Michelle A. Meade, "Disparities in Access to Health Care Among Adults with Physical Disabilities: Analysis of a Representative National Sample for a Ten-Year Period," *ScienceDirect*, April 2015. https://www.sciencedirect.com/science/article/abs/pii/S193665741400106X?via%3Dihub.

100 *adults with congenital defects:* Gloria L. Krahn, Deborah Klein Walker, and Rosaly Correa-De-Araujo, "Persons with Disabilities as an Unrecognized Health Disparity Population," *American Journal of Public*

Health, April 2015. https://www.ncbi.nlm.nih.gov/pmc/articles/PMC4355692/.

101 *top billionaires graduated from college:* Deniz Çam, "Doctorate, Degree or Dropout: How Much Education It Takes to Become a Billionaire," *Forbes*, October 18, 2017. https://www.forbes.com/sites/denizcam/2017/10/18/doctorate-degree-or-dropout-how-much-education-it-takes-to-become-a-billionaire/?sh=28dd45c6b044.

102 *more likely to live in poverty:* Richard Fry, "5 Facts About Millennial Households," Pew Research Center, September 6, 2017. https://www.pewresearch.org/short-reads/2017/09/06/5-facts-about-millennial-households/.

102 *drowning in student loan debt:* Alexandre Tanzi, "Gen Z Has Worse Student Debt than Millennials," Bloomberg.com, August 26, 2022. https://www.bloomberg.com/news/articles/2022-08-26/gen-z-student-debt-worse-than-millennials-st-louis-fed-says#xj4y7vzkg.

105 *"irrational" optimism:* Sandee LaMotte, "Do Optimists Live Longer? Of Course They Do," CNN, June 9, 2022. https://www.cnn.com/2022/06/09/health/living-longer-optimist-study-wellness/index.html#:~:text=A%20growing%20body%20of%20research&text=A%202019%20study%20found%20both,to%20age%2085%20or%20beyond.

105 *Siddhartha Mukherjee:* Decca Aitkenhead, "Siddhartha Mukherjee: 'A Positive Attitude Does Not Cure Cancer, Any More than a Negative One Causes It,'" *The Guardian*, December 4, 2011. https://www.theguardian.com/books/2011/dec/04/siddhartha-mukherjee-talk-about-cancer.

6. Time to Spiral

108 *unclassified UAP documents:* Gregg Eghigian, "UFOs, UAPs—Whatever We Call Them, Why Do We Assume Mysterious Flying Objects Are Extraterrestrial?," *Smithsonian*, August 5, 2021. https://www.smithsonianmag.com/air-space-magazine/ufos-uapswhatever-we-call-them-why-do-we-assume-mysterious-flying-objects-are-extraterrestrial-180978374/.

115 *attention span, speed, and low-quality news:* Jenny Odell, *How to Do Nothing: Resisting the Attention Economy* (New York: Melville House, 2021).

117 *physiological power:* Richard F. Mollica and Thomas Hübl, "Numb from the News? Understanding Why and What to Do May Help," *Harvard Health*, March 18, 2021. https://

www.health.harvard.edu/blog/numb-from-the-news-understanding-why-and-what-to-do-may-help-2021031822176.

119 *Studies of phone addiction:* Trevor Haynes, "Dopamine, Smartphones & You: A Battle for Your Time," Harvard University, Science in the News, May 1, 2018. https://sitn.hms.harvard.edu/flash/2018/dopamine-smartphones-battle-time/.

120 *caused the global attention span to shrink:* "Abundance of Information Narrows Our Collective Attention Span," *EurekAlert!*, April 15, 2019. https://www.eurekalert.org/news-releases/490177.

120 *Sune Lehmann, one of the study's authors:* Dream McClinton, "Global Attention Span Is Narrowing and Trends Don't Last as Long, Study Reveals," *The Guardian*, April 17, 2019. https://www.theguardian.com/society/2019/apr/16/got-a-minute-global-attention-span-is-narrowing-study-reveals.

121 *urgent-vs.-important matrix:* Peter Drucker, *The Effective Executive* (New York: HarperCollins, 1966).

122 *time's wondrous pliancy:* Virginia Woolf, *Orlando* (New York: Crosby Gaige, 1928).

122 *Albert Einstein wrote a letter:* "Resetting the Theory of Time," NPR, May 17, 2013. https://www.npr.org/2013/05/17/184775924/resetting-the-theory-of-time#:~:text=Albert%20Einstein%20once%20wrote%3A%20People,that%20true%20reality%20is%20timeless.

124 *Jupiter year:* "How Long Is a Year on Other Planets?," *SpacePlace*, July 13, 2020. https://spaceplace.nasa.gov/years-on-other-planets/en/.

124 *quarantime was distorted:* Ruth S. Ogden, "The Passage of Time During the UK Covid-19 Lockdown," *PLOS One*, July 6, 2020. https://journals.plos.org/plosone/article?id=10.1371%2Fjournal.pone.0235871.

125 *awe is the kind of humbling wonder:* David Keltner, *Awe: The New Science of Everyday Wonder and How It Can Transform Your Life* (New York: Penguin, 2023).

125 *Simply looking at nature:* Stacey Kennelly, "Can Awe Buy You More Time and Happiness?," *DailyGood*, December 3, 2012. https://www.dailygood.org/story/353/can-awe-buy-you-more-time-and-happiness-stacey-kennelly/.

125 *awe as an artistic tool*: Rick Rubin, *The Creative Act: A Way of Being* (New York: Penguin, 2023).

126 *"time disappears"*: Alice Robb, "The 'Flow State': Where Creative Work Thrives," *BBC Worklife*, February 5, 2022. https://www.bbc.com/worklife/article/20190204-how-to-find-your-flow-state-to-be-peak-creative.

126 *hyperfocus on sensory moments:* Marc Wittmann et al., "Subjective Expansion of Extended Time-Spans in Experienced Meditators," *Frontiers in Psychology* 5 (2015). https://doi.org/10.3389/fpsyg.2014.01586.

126 *eight weeks of mindfulness lessons:* Elizabeth A. Hoge et al., "Mindfulness-Based Stress Reduction vs. Escitalopram for the Treatment of Adults with Anxiety Disorders," *JAMA Psychiatry* 80, no. 1 (2023). https://doi.org/10.1001/jamapsychiatry.2022.3679.

127 *taking walks in nature:* Mariya Davydenko, "Time Grows on Trees: The Effect of Nature Settings on Time Perception," *Journal of Environmental Psychology* 54 (December 2017): 20–26. https://doi.org/10.22215/etd/2017-11962.

127 *"Perhaps wilderness is an antidote":* Nicholas Kristof, "Blissfully Lost in the Woods," *New York Times*, July 28, 2012. https://www.nytimes.com/2012/07/29/opinion/sunday/kristof-blissfully-lost-in-the-woods.html.

7. The Scammer Within

129 *held up the tellers at gunpoint:* Sam Brinson, "Is Overconfidence Tearing the World Apart?," Sam Brinson. Accessed September 8, 2023. https://www.sambrinson.com/overconfidence/.

132 *Dunning-Kruger effect:* Justin Kruger and David Dunning, "Unskilled and Unaware of It: How Difficulties in Recognizing One's Own Incompetence Lead to Inflated Self-Assessments," *Journal of Personality and Social Psychology* 77, no. 6 (1999): 1121–34. https://doi.org/10.1037/0022-3514.77.6.1121.

132 *an interview with McGill University:* Jonathan Jarry, "The Dunning-Kruger Effect Is Probably Not Real," McGill University Office for Science and Society, December 17, 2020. https://www.mcgill.ca/oss/article/critical-thinking/dunning-kruger-effect-probably-not-real.

133 *coining in the 1960s:* Scott Plous, "Chapter 19: Overconfidence," in *The Psychology of Judgment and Decision Making* (New York: McGraw-Hill Higher Education, 2007).

133 *research on superiority complexes:* Makiko Yamada et al., "Superiority Illusion Arises from Resting-State Brain Networks Modulated by Do-

NOTES

pamine," *Proceedings of the National Academy of Sciences* 110, no. 11 (2013): 4363–67. https://doi.org/10.1073/pnas.1221681110.

134 *famous 1981 study:* Ola Svenson, "Are We All Less Risky and More Skillful Than Our Fellow Drivers?," *Acta Psychologica* 47, no. 2 (February 1981): 143–48. https://doi.org/10.1016/0001-6918(81)90005-6.

135 *natural selection may have favored a swollen ego:* Dominic D. P. Johnson and James H. Fowler, "The Evolution of Overconfidence," *Nature News*, September 14, 2011. https://www.nature.com/articles/nature10384/.

135 *"blind one to the possibility of failure":* Roger Lowenstein, *When Genius Failed* (London: Fourth Estate, 2002).

136 *argued UC Berkeley psychologist Cameron Anderson:* Claire Shipman and Katty Kay, "The Confidence Gap," *The Atlantic*, May 2014. https://www.theatlantic.com/magazine/archive/2014/05/the-confidence-gap/359815/.

136 *"self-deceptive bluffing":* Kun Li, Rui Cong, Te Wu, and Long Wang, "Bluffing Promotes Overconfidence on Social Networks," *Scientific Reports* 4, no. 1 (2014). https://doi.org/10.1038/srep05491.

137 *desire to be internet famous:* "Most Kids Want to Be Social Media Influencers, Is It Realistic?," abc10.com, February 22, 2022. https://www.abc10.com/video/entertainment/most-kids-want-to-be-social-media-influencers-is-it-realistic/103-fc9d8b19-60c1-43a1-a774-8b5927e65244.

137 *as many British, Chinese, and American children:* Natalya Saldanha, "In 2018, an 8-Year-Old Made $22 Million on YouTube. No Wonder Kids Want to Be Influencers," *Fast Company*, November 19, 2019. https://www.fastcompany.com/90432765/why-do-kids-want-to-be-influencers.

138 *overconfident CEOs:* Josie Rhodes Cook, "Bad News, Elon Musk: Overconfident CEOS Have a Higher Risk of Being Sued," *Inverse*, August 29, 2018. https://www.inverse.com/article/48486-overconfident-ceos-are-more-likely-to-get-sued-study-says.

141 *certain types of narcissists:* Scott Barry Kaufman, "Are Narcissists More Likely to Experience Impostor Syndrome?," Scientific American Blog Network, September 11, 2018. https://blogs.scientificamerican.com/beautiful-minds/are-narcissists-more-likely-to-experience-impostor-syndrome/#:~:text=Vulnerable%20narcissists%20have%20an%20incessant,as%20they%20believe%20they%20are.

142 *American labor market:* Shahamat Uddin, "Racism Runs Deep in Professionalism Culture," *The Tulane Hullabaloo*, January 23,

2020. https://tulanehullabaloo.com/51652/intersections/business-professionalism-is-racist/.

143 *women were viewed as less moral:* Sarah J. Ward and Laura A. King, "Gender Differences in Emotion Explain Women's Lower Immoral Intentions and Harsher Moral Condemnation," *Personality and Social Psychology Bulletin* 44, no. 5 (January 2018): 653–69. https://doi.org/10.1177/0146167217744525.

144 *"who throw the first stones":* Elliot Aronson and Carol Tavris, *Mistakes Were Made (But Not by Me)* (New York: HarperCollins, 2020).

145 *The 2017 book:* Steven Sloman and Philip Fernbach, *The Knowledge Illusion* (New York: Riverhead Books, 2017).

145 *So smooth is our cooperation:* Elizabeth Kolbert, "Why Facts Don't Change Our Minds," *The New Yorker*, February 19, 2017. https://www.newyorker.com/magazine/2017/02/27/why-facts-dont-change-our-minds.

146 *Audre Lorde said:* Audre Lorde, "Poetry Is Not a Luxury," We Tip the Balance. Accessed September 21, 2023. http://wetipthebalance.org/wp-content/uploads/2015/07/Poetry-is-Not-a-Luxury-Audre-Lorde.pdf.

147 *humility:* "APA Dictionary of Psychology," American Psychological Association. Accessed September 11, 2023. https://dictionary.apa.org/humility.

148 *when confidence is well aligned with performance:* Max Rollwage and Stephen M. Fleming, "Confirmation Bias Is Adaptive When Coupled with Efficient Metacognition," *Philosophical Transactions of the Royal Society B: Biological Sciences* 376, no. 1822 (2021). Accessed September 11, 2023. https://doi.org/10.1098/rstb.2020.0131.

148 *war game experiments:* Dominic D. Johnson, Nils B. Weidmann, and Lars-Erik Cederman, "Fortune Favours the Bold: An Agent-Based Model Reveals Adaptive Advantages of Overconfidence in War," *PLOS One* 6, no. 6 (June 24, 2011). https://doi.org/10.1371/journal.pone.0020851.

8. Haters Are My Motivators

152 *lore from the Middle Ages:* "The Middle Ages," *Encyclopædia Britannica*. Accessed September 11, 2023. https://www.britannica.com/topic/government/Representation-and-constitutional-monarchy.

153 *A much circulated 2019 headline:* Lynn Parramore, "The Average American Worker Takes Less Vacation Time Than a Medieval Peasant," *Business Insider*, November 7, 2016. https://

NOTES

www.businessinsider.com/american-worker-less-vacation-medieval-peasant-2016-11.

154 *illusory truth effect:* "Why Do We Believe Misinformation More Easily When It's Repeated Many Times?," The Decision Lab. Accessed September 11, 2023. https://thedecisionlab.com/biases/illusory-truth-effect.

155 *they rely on simple heuristics:* Alice H. Eagly and Shelly Chaiken, *The Psychology of Attitudes* (New York: Harcourt Brace Jovanovich College Publishers, 1993).

156 Dr. Moiya McTier, *The Milky Way: An Autobiography of Our Galaxy* (New York: Grand Central Publishing, 2023).

156 *college students fell prey to the illusory truth effect:* Lisa K. Fazio, Elizabeth J. Marsh, Nadia M. Brashier, and B. Keith Payne, "Knowledge Does Not Protect Against Illusory Truth," *Journal of Experimental Psychology* 144, no. 5 (2015): 993–1002. https://doi.org/10.1037/e520562012-049.

157 *a survey on illusory truth using fake-news headlines:* Gordon Pennycook, Tyrone D. Cannon, and David G. Rand, "Prior Exposure Increases Perceived Accuracy of Fake News," *Journal of Experimental Psychology*, 2017. https://doi.org/10.2139/ssrn.2958246.

160 *online social lore surrounding perceived "moochers":* Tom Mould, "Counter Memes and Anti-Legends in Online Welfare Discourse," *Journal of American Folklore* 135, no. 538 (2022): 441–65. https://doi.org/10.5406/15351882.135.538.03.

161 *perceive information as more believable:* Aumyo Hassan and Sarah J. Barber, "The Effects of Repetition Frequency on the Illusory Truth Effect," *Cognitive Research: Principles and Implications* 6, no. 1 (May 13, 2021). https://doi.org/10.1186/s41235-021-00301-5.

161 *rhyme-as-reason effect:* Itamar Shatz, "The Rhyme-as-Reason Effect: Why Rhyming Makes Messages More Persuasive," Effectiviology. Accessed September 11, 2023. https://effectiviology.com/rhyme-as-reason/.

161 *Rhyme feels extra impactful in English:* Arika Okrent, "Why Is the English Spelling System So Weird and Inconsistent?: Aeon Essays," Edited by Sally Davies, *Aeon*, July 26, 2021. https://aeon.co/essays/why-is-the-english-spelling-system-so-weird-and-inconsistent.

162 *"acoustic encoding":* Kathryn Devine, "Why You Should Take the Time to Rhyme: The Rhyme as Reason Effect," *CogBlog—A Cognitive Psychology Blog*, November 26, 2019. https://web.colby.edu/cogblog

NOTES

/2019/11/26/why-you-should-take-the-time-to-rhyme-the-rhyme-as-reason-effect/.

162 *"purifies the basics":* Gina Kolata, "Rhyme's Reason: Linking Thinking to Train the Brain?," *New York Times*, February 19, 1995. https://www.nytimes.com/1995/02/19/weekinreview/ideas-trends-rhyme-s-reason-linking-thinking-to-train-the-brain.html.

162 *Barbara Tversky observed:* Barbara Tversky, "The Cognitive Design of Tools of Thought," *Review of Philosophy and Psychology* 6, no. 1 (2014): 99–116. https://doi.org/10.1007/s13164-014-0214-3.

163 *"Keats heuristic":* Matthew S. McGlone and Jessica Tofighbakhsh, "The Keats Heuristic: Rhyme as Reason in Aphorism Interpretation," *Poetics* 26, no. 4 (1999): 235–44. https://doi.org/10.1016/s0304-422x(99)00003-0.

163 *the work of Hunter College psychology professor:* Tracy Dennis-Tiwary, *Future Tense: Why Anxiety Is Good for You (Even Though It Feels Bad)* (New York: Harper Wave, 2022).

165 *Jill Bolte Taylor is interviewed:* "A World Without Words," *Radiolab*, n.d.

165 *her bestselling memoir:* Jill Bolte Taylor, *My Stroke of Insight: A Brain Scientist's Personal Journey* (New York: Penguin, 2006).

167 *poetry collection:* Rebecca Elson, *A Responsibility to Awe* (Manchester, UK: Carcanet Classics, 2018).

9. Sorry I'm Late, Must Be Mercury in Retrograde

170 *sporting arms of irregular tininess:* Matt Blitz, "Jurassic Park Lied to You: T-Rex Had Great Eyesight Really," *Gizmodo*, May 16, 2014. https://gizmodo.com/jurassic-park-lied-to-you-t-rex-had-great-eyesight-rea-1577352103.

174 *One of my favorite books on confirmation bias:* Elliot Aronson and Carol Tavris, *Mistakes Were Made (But Not by Me)* (New York: HarperCollins, 2020).

176 *Santa Ana winds:* Joan Didion, *Slouching Towards Bethlehem* (New York: Farrar, Straus & Giroux, 1968).

177 *something called "Y2K":* Mitch Ratcliffe, "Y2K Survivalists Struggle with Reality," UPI, January 2, 2000. https://www.upi.com/Archives/2000/01/02/Y2K-survivalists-struggle-with-reality/8815946789200/.

179 *the bias's evolutionary benefits:* Uwe Peters, "What Is the Function of Confirmation Bias?," *Erkenntnis* 87, no. 3 (April 20, 2020): 1351–76. https://doi.org/10.1007/s10670-020-00252-1.

181 *classic 1979 Stanford study:* Charles G. Lord, Lee Ross, and Mark R. Lepper. "Biased Assimilation and Attitude Polarization: The Effects of Prior Theories on Subsequently Considered Evidence." *Journal of Personality and Social Psychology* 37, no. 11 (November 1979): 2098–2109. https://doi.org/10.1037/0022-3514.37.11.2098.

181 *climate change perceptions:* Ronald Bailey, "Climate Change and Confirmation Bias," Reason.com, July 12, 2011. https://reason.com/2011/07/12/scientific-literacy-climate-ch/.

182 *prescient post-apocalyptic novel:* Emily St. John Mandel, *Station Eleven* (New York: Alfred A. Knopf, 2014).

182 *A 2021 study:* Max Rollwage and Stephen M. Fleming, "Confirmation Bias Is Adaptive When Coupled with Efficient Metacognition," *Philosophical Transactions of the Royal Society B: Biological Sciences* 376, no. 1822 (2021). Accessed September 11, 2023. https://doi.org/10.1098/rstb.2020.0131.

10. Nostalgia Porn

185 *discussions of flow states:* Mihaly Csikszentmihalyi, "Flow, the Secret to Happiness," TED Talks, February 2004. https://www.ted.com/talks/mihaly_csikszentmihalyi_flow_the_secret_to_happiness/transcript.

185 *self-reported super-content Americans:* Arthur C. Brooks, "Free People Are Happy People," *City Journal*, Spring 2008. https://www.city-journal.org/article/free-people-are-happy-people.

186 *"anemoia":* John Koenig, *The Dictionary of Obscure Sorrows* (New York: Simon & Schuster, 2021).

187 *"Past events exist":* Ursula K. Le Guin, *Tales from Earthsea* (New York: Harcourt, 2001).

188 *declinism:* "Why Do We Think the Past Is Better than the Future?," The Decision Lab. Accessed September 11, 2023. https://thedecisionlab.com/biases/declinism.

188 *fading affect bias:* W. Richard Walker and John J. Skowronski, "The Fading Affect Bias: But What the Hell Is It For?," *Applied Cognitive Psychology* 23, no. 8 (2009): 1122–36. https://doi.org/10.1002/acp.1614.

NOTES

190 *A 2015 UCLA psychology study:* Cynthia Lee, "The Stranger Within: Connecting with Our Future Selves," UCLA, April 9, 2015. https://newsroom.ucla.edu/stories/the-stranger-within-connecting-with-our-future-selves.

190 *freaky CGI version: Lady and the Tramp*, Walt Disney Studios Motion Pictures, 2019.

191 *the park was originally built:* Eric Avila, "Popular Culture in the Age of White Flight: Film Noir, Disneyland, and the Cold War (Sub)Urban Imaginary," *Journal of Urban History* 31, no. 1 (November 2004): 3–22. https://doi.org/10.1177/0096144204266745.

191 *the culture's renewed embrace of Dolly Parton:* Tressie McMillan Cottom, "The Dolly Moment: Why We Stan a Post-Racism Queen," tressie.substack.com – essaying, February 24, 2021. https://tressie.substack.com/p/the-dolly-moment.

192 *supposed "Golden Age":* Ben Carlson, "Golden Age Thinking," A Wealth of Common Sense, December 31, 2020. https://awealthofcommonsense.com/2020/12/golden-age-thinking/.

193 *negativity bias:* Elizabeth Whitworth, "Declinism Bias: Why People Think the Sky Is Falling—Shortform," *Shortform*, September 17, 2022. https://www.shortform.com/blog/declinism-bias/.

194 *"catastrophe fatigue":* Sasha Lilley, David McNally, Eddie Yuen, and James Davis, *Catastrophism* (Binghamton, NY: PM Press, 2012).

195 *dropping exponentially for decades:* Max Roser, "Proof That Life Is Getting Better for Humanity, in 5 Charts," *Vox*, December 23, 2016.

196 *She quoted James Baldwin:* "A Conversation with James Baldwin," June 24, 1963, WGBH, American Archive of Public Broadcasting (GBH and the Library of Congress), Boston, MA, and Washington, DC. Accessed September 11, 2023. http://americanarchive.org/catalog/cpb-aacip-15-0v89g5gf5r.

196 *It's hard to OD on freedom:* Carol Graham, "Are Women Happier than Men? Do Gender Rights Make a Difference?," Brookings, August 2020. https://www.brookings.edu/articles/are-women-happier-than-men-do-gender-rights-make-a-difference/.

197 *James Davies noted:* James Davies, *Sedated: How Modern Capitalism Caused Our Mental Health Crisis* (London: Atlantic Books, 2021).

199 *there's been a shift in her field:* "The Cult of Fast Fashion," *Sounds Like a Cult*, May 17, 2022. https://open.spotify.com/episode/1LfqDsztUy6RPiiONn0dek.

NOTES

11. The Life-Changing Magic of Becoming a Mediocre Crafter

207 *IKEA effect:* Jennifer Clinehens, "The IKEA Effect: How the Psychology of Co-Creation Hooks Customers," *Medium*, January 5, 2020. https://medium.com/choice-hacking/how-the-psychology-of-co-creation-hooks-customers-330570f115.

207 *demonstrated the intrinsic urge:* Michael I. Norton, Daniel Mochon, and Dan Ariely, "The 'IKEA Effect': When Labor Leads to Love," *Journal of Consumer Psychology* 22 (2011): 453–60. https://doi.org/10.2139/ssrn.1777100.

209 *eggy legend:* Gary Mortimer, Frank Mathmann, and Louise Grimmer, "The IKEA Effect: How We Value the Fruits of Our Labour over Instant Gratification," *The Conversation*, April 18, 2019. https://theconversation.com/the-ikea-effect-how-we-value-the-fruits-of-our-labour-over-instant-gratification-113647.

209 *up for debate:* David Mikkelson, "Requiring an Egg Made Instant Cake Mixes Sell?," Snopes, January 30, 2008. https://www.snopes.com/fact-check/something-eggstra/.

210 *the crowdfunding industry:* Ivy Taylor, "Over Three Times as Many Video Game Projects Fail than Succeed on Kickstarter," *GamesIndustry.biz*, October 24, 2017. https://www.gamesindustry.biz/success-of-resident-evil-2-board-game-paints-a-curious-picture-of-kickstarter-in-2017.

211 *"languishing":* Adam Grant, "There's a Name for the Blah You're Feeling: It's Called Languishing," *New York Times*, April 19, 2021. https://www.nytimes.com/2021/04/19/well/mind/covid-mental-health-languishing.html.

212 *2023 analysis of American time use:* Andrew Van Dam, "The Happiest, Least Stressful, Most Meaningful Jobs in America," *Washington Post*, January 6, 2023. https://www.washingtonpost.com/business/2023/01/06/happiest-jobs-on-earth/.

214 *Needles and fabric do wonders for the spirit:* Michelle Borst Polino, "Crochet Therapy," Counseling. Accessed September 21, 2023. https://www.counseling.org/docs/default-source/aca-acc-creative-activities-clearinghouse/crochet-therapy.pdf?sfvrsn=6.

215 *AI-generated art:* Gabe Cohn, "AI Art at Christie's Sells for $432,500," *New York Times*, October 25, 2018. https://www.nytimes.com/2018/10/25/arts/design/ai-art-sold-christies.html.

NOTES

215 *"Monkey Christ":* Hannah Jane Parkinson, "It's a Botch-Up! Monkey Christ and the Worst Art Repairs of All Time," *The Guardian*, June 24, 2020. https://www.theguardian.com/artanddesign/2020/jun/24/monkey-christ-worst-art-repairs-of-all-time.

216 *a fan of the Australian musician Nick Cave wrote in to his blog:* Nick Cave, "Considering Human Imagination the Last Piece of Wilderness, Do You Think AI Will Ever Be Able to Write a Good Song?," *The Red Hand Files*. January 2019, https://www.theredhandfiles.com/considering-human-imagination-the-last-piece-of-wilderness-do-you-think-ai-will-ever-be-able-to-write-a-good-song/.

217 *called our judgments:* Claire L. Evans, "The Sound of (Posthuman) Music," *Vice*, May 14, 2014. https://www.vice.com/en/article/bmjmkz/the-sound-of-posthuman-music.

218 *reference the era's major political conflicts:* William F. Claire, "That Rare, Random Descent: The Poetry and Pathos of Sylvia Plath," *The Antioch Review* 26, no. 4 (1966): 552–60. https://doi.org/10.2307/4610812.

INDEX

A

absorption addiction model of celebrity worship, 24
accuracy
    fluency vs., 155
    repetition vs., 156–157
    timeliness vs., 180–181
acoustic encoding, 162
activism
    celebrity activism, 16
    creativity and, 146
additive solution bias, 63–64
adolescents
    aspirations to emulate media figures, 15
    and celebrity worship, 15–16
    celebrity worship vs. worship of adults they know, 24
"Africa" (Weezer cover of Toto song), 210–211
AI-generated art and music, 215–217
allegory, 165–166
Alternative for Germany party, 192
alternative mental health influencers, 38, 46–48
    see also "Manifestation Doctor, The"
Alwyn, Joe, 20
American Medical Association Code of Ethics, 45
American Psychological Association, humility defined by, 147
Americans
    and conspiracy theories, 32–33
    evolution of celebrity worship, 16, 17
    and fake news, 44–45
    growth in mistrust of government, 16, 17
    internet fame as adolescent goal, 137
    overconfidence bias, 131
    percentage who report their life is "very happy," 185–186
    socioeconomic conditions for individuals with disabilities, 100–101
    socioeconomic status and susceptibility to zero-sum bias, 78
    student debt, 102
amygdala, 60, 117–118
anastasis, 167
Anderson, Cameron, 136
"and then" storytelling, 103
anemoia, 186–188, 198
animism, 48–49
antifeminists, 189
anxiety(-ies)
    celebrities and, 84
    nostalgia as response to, 187
    origins in Middle Ages, 163–164
    paranoid thinking perpetuated by, 45
aphorisms, 159–160

INDEX

apocalypse
  and confirmation bias, 176–178
  and declinism, 194–195
Aral, Sinan, 44
Aronson, Elliot, 144, 174–175
astrology, 179
attention
  and flow, 126
  frequency bias as attention filter, 49–50
  information overload as cause of decline in attention span, 120–121
  and recency illusion, 115–116
avenoir, 197
awe, 216

B

B., Minaa, 105–106, 120
Baader-Meinhof phenomenon, 49
baby boomers, 16
backfire effect, 175
Baldwin, James, on optimism, 196
barter, 75
Beatles, the, 16
beauty industry
  and recency illusion, 116
  and zero-sum fallacy, 70–73, 76–79, 86
Beck, Koa, 143–144
Bernstein, Gabrielle, 37–38
Besso, Michele, 122
Betty Crocker instant cake mixes, 208–209
Beyoncé, 21, 88
billionaires, survivorship bias and, 100–102
Bock, Sheila, 160
bouquets, bridal, in Middle Ages, 151–154

Boyer, Pascal, 75
brain
  amygdala, 60, 117–118
  prefrontal cortex, 117, 174–175
brain cancer, 91
brain function, 117–120
brain scans, 197
brands
  as communities, 211
  and proportionality bias, 211
bridal bouquets, in Middle Ages, 151–154
Brogan, Kelly, 41
Bush, George W., 174
"but/therefore" storytelling, 103
Byrne, Rhonda, 39n

C

cake mixes, 208–209
cancer
  in children, 40
  Denise Montell's experience, 13, 167
  and survivorship bias, 90–95, 98–101, 105
  vlogging by cancer patients, 90–95, 99–106
cannibalism, 27
capitalism
  and breakups as "failures," 62
  and materialism, 197
  and zero-sum bias, 75–76, 82
Casey (author's partner), *see* Kolb, Casey
Castellano, Mattia, 92
Castellano, Talia Joy, 91–93, 105, 106
catastrophe fatigue, 194–195
Catastrophism (Yuen, et al.), 194–195
catharsis, connection as, 89

INDEX

catharsis hypothesis, 83
cause and effect, survivorship bias's fundamental misunderstanding of, 102–103
Cave, Nick, 216
celebrities
   comeback stories and nostalgia, 191–192
   and jealousy, 84
celebrity worship
   categories of, 19
   in China, 24
   increase (2000–2021), 15
   origin of "fan" as term, 16
   social media's amplifying effect on, 17–18
   standom and, 18–19
   stans' reactions to betrayal, 24–25
Center for Countering Digital Hate, 41
CEOs, overconfidence bias and, 137–138
Chaiken, Shelly, 155
Challenger space shuttle disaster, 138
Charlemagne, 153
"Charli's Angels," 21–22
Charli XCX, 21–22
childhood cancer, 40
China, celebrity worship by teenagers in, 24
Choe, David, 37
Christian fundamentalism, 171–172, 176
circadian rhythms, 122
clickbait, 116–118
climate crisis
   declinism and, 193–194
   scientific literacy's effect on perceptions of, 181–182
clinical depression, *see* depression

cognitive biases
   defined, 3
   as social illusion, 110
   see also specific biases, e.g.: confirmation bias
Colin-Thome, Danielle, 18
Columbia University fighter plane armor study (1943), 96–97
confirmation bias, 173–184
connection
   as antidote to toxic stress, 87–89
   IKEA effect and, 213
conspiracy theories
   conspirituality and, 48
   COVID-19 and, 33
   "Manifestation Doctor" and, 42–43
   proportionality bias and, 29, 34–35
   and self-healing, 42
   spiritual pseudopsychology and, 46–47
conspiracy theorists, 34
conspiracy therapy, 39
conspirituality, 33, 49
consumerism, additive solution bias and, 64
Cottom, Tressie McMillan, 191
Courtney (cancer patient), 91, 92n–93n
COVID-19
   and conspiracy theories, 33
   and "languishing," 211
   perception of time during lockdown, 124–126
   self-help programs during pandemic, 37
   Sean Whalen's view of, 42
crafts, 203–205
   see also IKEA effect
Creative Act, The: A Way of Being, 125–126

INDEX

crime, overconfidence bias and, 129–130, 138
crowdfunding, 210
Csikszentmihalyi, Mihaly, 126, 185, 196
Cultish (Montell), 174
cults
   confirmation bias among members, 174, 181
   and irrationality, 3
   and love-bombing, 66
   toxic relationships' similarities to, 57, 65–69
cystic fibrosis, 92

D

Davies, James, 197
"Day After My Diagnosis with Cancer, The" (vlog), 95
deaths of despair, 196*n*
decision-making, confirmation bias as aid in, 180–181
declinism, 188–201
   defined, 188
   populism and, 192–193
defeatism, 194
dehumanization, as cult behavior, 66–67
Dennis-Tiwary, Tracy, 163–164
depression
   and depressive realism, 133*n*
   self-assessment and, 133–134
   upward social comparison and, 81
"devaluation" phase of unhealthy partnership, 66–67
Dictionary of Obscure Sorrows, The (Koenig), 195, 197
Didion, Joan
   on information, 53
   proportionality bias in behavior after husband's death, 5
   on Santa Ana winds, 176
   and superstition, 36
DiNardo, Dena, 41, 45, 85–87
dinosaurs, 169–172, 183–184
"discard" phase of unhealthy partnership, 66–67
Discord, 37
disgust, illusory truth effect and, 163
"Disinformation Dozen" 41
divorce, 62
DIY culture, 209–210
   see also IKEA effect
"Dolly Moment, The: Why We Stan a Post Racism Queen" (Cottom), 191
Doody, Ryan, 59–61
"doomers," 177, 178
doomsday, *see* apocalypse
Drucker, Peter, on efficiency vs. effectiveness, 121
Dunning, David, 131–132
Dunning–Kruger effect, 132
Durvasula, Ramani, 58, 66–67

E

Eagly, Alice, 155
East Asians, 78
ecstasy, 126
Edmond de Belamy (AI-generated artwork), 215–216
Effective Executive, The (Drucker), 121
efficiency, effectiveness vs., 121
effort justification bias
   IKEA effect and, 212–213
   see also sunk cost fallacy
ego, *see* overconfidence bias
Einstein, Albert, 122
election of 2016
   fake news and illusory truth effect, 157
   and zero-sum bias, 78

INDEX

Elson, Rebecca, 167
Eminem, 9
empathic concern, 143
employment, self-worth and, 211–212
Enlightenment, the, 164
Ephron, Nora, 203
Epstein, Mark, 22
Eras Tour (Taylor Swift), 23–24
evangelicals, 171–172, 176
Evans, Claire L., 217
Ewing's sarcoma, 98–99
Extended Mind, The (Paul), 183

F

Facebook, conspiratorial headlines on, 157–158
fading affect bias, 188
fake news, 157
Fanon, Frantz, 2–3
fans/fandom, *see* celebrity worship
Fazio, Lisa, 156–157
feminism
   and capitalism, 82
   and nostalgia, 191–192
   and tradwives, 189
Fernbach, Philip, 145
fighter plane armor study (1943), 96–97
fluency, accuracy vs., 155
folk economics, 75
folklore, illusory truth effect and, 158–160, 166
folk tales, 153
Food and Drug Administration, 45
40-hour work week, 141–142
France, far-right nationalism in, 192
freedom, happiness and, 196–197
frequency bias, 49–50
Freud, Sigmund, 83
Friedman, Ann, 88

frontal lobe, 86–87
fundamentalism, 171–172, 176
furniture-flipping, 205–207
Future Tense: Why Anxiety Is Good for You (Even Though It Feels Bad) (Dennis-Tiwary), 163–164

G

Gall, Sophia, 92, 93, 102–106
gay males, misogynistic engagement with female pop icons by, 25
gender disparities
   imposter syndrome and, 140–141
   and zero-sum bias, 81–82
General Mills, 208
Gen Z, student loan debt and, 102
Germany, right-wing nationalism in, 192–193
Getty Museum, 97–98
Giles, Laura, 48–49
"Goldilocks Zone," 167
"good enough mother," 26–27
Good Morning America, 21
Google
   and illusory truth effect, 157–158
   and overconfidence bias, 146
Goop, 41
Graham, Carol, 196*n*
Grant, Adam, 211
Great Depression, 70–71
Greece, ancient, 186
Grose, Jessica, 5, 16–17
Gutowitz, Jill, 20

H

Haidt, Jonathan, 87
halo effect, 11–27
   and celebrity worship, 15–16
   defined, 11–12

INDEX

happiness, quality of life vs., 196
Heather ("Manifestation Doctor" follower), 42–44
heuristics, 155
Hitler, Adolf, 192–193
hobbies, 203–204
Hodgkin's lymphoma, 93
"holistic self-empowerment," 30
Holmes, Elizabeth, 131, 140
homesteading influencers, 204–205
hooks, bell, 6
hope, limits of, 104
horoscopes, 179
How to Do Nothing: Resisting the Attention Economy (Odell), 115
humility, 146–147

I

identity formation, social comparison and, 85
IKEA effect, 207–215
  defined, 207–208
  positive aspects of, 213–214
illnesses, vlogging of, 90–93
illusory truth effect, 154–167
immigration policies, zero-sum bias and, 78
imposter syndrome, 139–142
individualism, zero-sum bias and, 76–77
Industrial Revolution, 75
Information Age, 75–76
inspiration porn, 100
Instagram
  and celebrity culture, 17, 18
  effect on self-image, 73
  effect on young women, 82
  and identity development, 85
  and jealousy, 88–89
  mental health influencers on, 31, 38–39, 43
  morally judgmental women on, 144
  and social comparison, 85
  and zero-sum bias, 79, 82, 86, 98
instant cake mixes, 208–209
internet, *see* social media; specific platforms
"internet famous," 137
iPhone, 131
Isabel (homesteading influencers), 204–205

J

Jackson, Michael, 84–85
Janega, Eleanor, 152–153, 154n
January 6, 2021, U.S. Capitol invasion, 33
Japan, collectivism as prevailing attitude in, 77
jealousy, 79–80, 84
Jeha, Raigda, 92, 104–106
jobs, IKEA effect and, 211–212
Jobs, Steve, 131, 133
judgment
  human mind and, 60–61
  overconfidence bias and, 133, 137, 138
  survivorship bias's effect on, 97

K

Kahneman, Daniel, 3n
Keats, John, 163
Keats heuristic, 163
Keltner, Dacher, 125
Kerry, John, 174
knitting, 214n
knowledge
  Dunning-Kruger effect and, 132
  heuristics, 155

INDEX

and illusory truth effect, 156–158, 164
overconfidence bias about, 134
web searches and, 145–146
Knowledge Illusion, The (Fernbach and Sloman), 145
Knox, Amanda, 35–36
koans, 6–7
Koenig, John, 186, 195, 197
Kolb, Casey (author's partner)
   on AI-generated music, 216–217
   effect of love on perception of time, 122–123
   and nostalgia, 197–198
   on percentage of Americans who report their life is "very happy," 185
   and UAP video, 109–110
Krastev, Sekoul, 115, 119–120
Kristen (author's friend), 170–172, 175, 184
Kristof, Nicholas, 127

L

labor, IKEA effect and, 211–212
language
   of cults, 174
   recency illusion and, 111–114
"languishing," 211
laughter, illusory truth effect and, 163
law of attraction, 39
legends, core qualities of, 158–159
Le Guin, Ursula K., 187
Lehmann, Sune, 120
Leviev, Simon ("Tinder Swindler"), 131, 142
"like-kind exchanges," 75
Lions Not Sheep, 42
"lipstick effect," 70–71
Loch Ness Monster, 177*n*

Long, Amy, 10–11, 21
Lorde, Audre, 146
loss aversion, sunk cost fallacy and, 59
love, romantic, effect on perception of time, 122–123
love-bombing, 66
Lover (Taylor Swift), 20
Lowenstein, Roger, 135
Ludden, David, 73, 199
lymphoma, 13

M

Maddeaux, Sabrina, 25
Madden, Sidney, 18
Madoff, Bernie, 138, 142
magical thinking, defined, 5–6
"Make Germany Great Again," 193
malpractice, by mental health practitioners, 45–46
Mandel, Emily St. John, 182
manifestation
   and conspiracy theories, 29
   elements of, 49–50
"Manifestation Doctor, The" (fictitious name), 29–34, 41–44, 49
Marie Claire magazine, 90
Mary (cancer survivor), 98–99, 102, 103
Maté, Gabor, 51
materialism, 197
McAndrew, Frank, 180, 181
McTier, Moiya, 156, 166
meaning, human attempts to ascribe to natural phenomena, 50–51
media figures, 15
   see also celebrities; celebrity worship
Mellors, Coco, 190

INDEX

memory
  of negative vs. positive emotions, 188–189
  nostalgia and, 197
  rhyme and, 162–163
mental health
  decline between 1990s and 2021, 2
  malpractice in, 45–46
  "The Manifestation Doctor" and, 30–34
  see also alternative mental health influencers
Middle Ages, 151–154, 163–164
millennials, financial status of, 102
mindfulness, 126
misogyny, 25
Mistakes Were Made (But Not by Me) (Tavris and Aronson), 144, 174–175
"Mr. Backpack" (pseudonym), 53–59, 61–68, 175
"Monkey Christ," 215
Montell, Denise (author's mother)
  "anastasis" coined by, 167
  elements of celebrity worship in author's relationship with, 25–26
  and halo effect, 13–15
  and language used to describe cancer, 101
moral reproach, 143
mothering, 22
Mould, Tom
  on legends, 158–159
  on power of memorable phrasing, 166–167
  on "welfare queen" trope, 160–161
movies
  nostalgia for recent eras, 190–191
  and "Year of the Cannibal," 27

MRIs, prefrontal cortex imaged by, 174–175
Mukherjee, Siddhartha, 105
Munko, 37
Murthy, Vivek H., 87
My Stroke of Insight (Taylor), 165
Myth of Normal, The (Maté), 51
"Myths of the Middle Ages" (Getty museum exhibit), 97–98

N

nationalism, declinism and, 192–193
National Rally party (France), 192
natural selection, overconfidence and, 135
nature, walks in, 127
Naumburg, Carla, 27
negativity bias, 193
Nelson, Maggie, 189, 196
neuroblastoma, 91
New Age, 39–42
"New to You" (YouTube category), 111n
Northern Lights, 50–51
Norton, Michael I., 207
nostalgia, 97, 186–192, 197–198, 200–201

O

Obama, Michelle, 203
O'Connor, Peg, 100
Odell, Jenny, 115
Offit, Paul, 17
On Freedom (Nelson), 189
optimism, "irrational," 104
optimism practice, 105–106
Orlando (Woolf), 122
osteosarcoma, 92
overconfidence, 129–133
  advantages of, 135–137
  as mental posture, 142
  risks of, 137–138

INDEX

overconfidence bias, 133–149
overthinking, 6
Owen, Sir Richard, 184
Oz, Dr., 45

P

Paltrow, Gwyneth, 41
paranoia
    conspiracy theories and, 44–45
    as profitable disposition, 36–37
    proportionality bias and, 35–36
parental figures, halo effect and, 13–15
parent–child attachment, celebrity worship and, 22
Parton, Dolly, 191
patriarchy, zero-sum bias and, 82
Paul, Annie Murphy, 183
Peale, Norman Vincent, 39n
Pennycook, Gord, 157
Peoplehood (group therapy business), 37
personal narratives, illusory truth effect and, 165
personal responsibility, self-healing and, 40
Peters, Uwe, 179–180
Petersen, Michael Bang, 75
Petrusich, Amanda, 23
Phillips, Lacy, 37, 49
phone addiction, 119n
phonemes, 162
phones
    addiction, 119
    effect on teenagers, 87
physical disabilities, people with, 100–101
Pinker, Steven, 162
Pinterest, 210
"Pinterest Fails," 134
Plath, Sylvia, 72–73
Plous, Scott, 138

populism
    declinism and, 192–193
    and zero-sum bias, 78
positive thinking, longevity and, 104
poverty
    global decline in, 195
    millennials and, 102
Power of Positive Thinking, The (Peale), 39n
prefrontal cortex, 117, 174–175
preppers, 178n
present bias, 190
presidential election of 2016
    fake news and illusory truth effect, 157
    and zero-sum bias, 78
Prince, 84–85
processed food, 208
"Proof That Life Is Getting Better for Humanity, in 5 Charts" (Roser), 195
proportionality bias, 29–51
    alternative psychotherapy and, 48
    and sentencing, 35–36
    survivorship bias's parallels with, 102
Protestant capitalism, 62
proverbs, 159–160
psychological disorders
    and "The Manifestation Doctor," 30–34
    standom and, 18–19
Psychology of Attitudes, The (Eagly and Chaiken), 155
Psychology of Judgment and Decision Making, The (Plous), 138
psychospirituality, 31
psychotherapy malpractice, 45–46
Pulse nightclub shooting (Orlando, Florida), 119
Purohit, Kush, 50n

INDEX

Q
QAnon, 33, 42–43
"QAnon Shaman," 33
quality of life, relation of happiness to, 196

R
Racheli (cancer survivor), 90, 93–96, 102–103, 205–207
radical imagination, 199
radical optimism, 95
Radiolab (podcast), 165
Rapture, the, 176
rationalization, confirmation bias and, 172–173
Reagan, Ronald 17
recency illusion, 111–127
  defined, 111–112
  digital news and, 115–116
regret, 62
religion, 171–172
religious cults, 65
repetition
  accuracy vs., 156–157
  and illusory truth effect, 155
resource competition, 75
resource-rational, human mind as, 4
Responsibility to Awe, A (Elson), 167
rhyme, tropes and, 161–163
rhyme-as-reason effect, 161–163
Richards, Jared, 25
Rolling Stone, "Year of the Cannibal" declaration, 27
romantic relationships
  effect on perception of time, 122–123
  sunk cost fallacy and, 52–69
Roser, Max, 195
Rowland, Kelly, 88
Rubin, Rick, 125–126

S
Sagan, Carl, 165–166
Sanderville, Linda
  on freeing up stretches of media-free time, 199–200
  on preferring the present to the past, 198–199
Savage, Dan, 68–69
scandals, Taylor Swift and, 10–11
science
  confirmation bias and scientific literacy, 181–182
  and language of mythology, 167
  as source of anxiety, 164
Scientific Revolution, 164
Secret, The (Byrne), 39n
Sedated: How Modern Capitalism Created our Mental Health Crisis (Davies), 197
self-deceptive bluffing, 136
"Self-Empowerment Circle," 43–44
self-healing, 39–40
Shakespeare, William, 161
Shetty, Jay, 37, 38
"Shine Theory," 88
shit-talking, 80–84
  and "spontaneous trait transference," 83
  and zero-sum bias, 80–81
Six Feet Under (HBO series), 200
60 Minutes, 107–108
Sloman, Steven, 145
Slouching Towards Bethlehem (Didion), 176
"small fish in a large pond," 78
smartphones
  effect of phone addiction, 119
  effect on teenagers, 87
social comparisons
  social media and, 85
  and zero-sum bias, 81–82

254

INDEX

social connection
    as antidote to toxic stress, 87–89
    IKEA effect and, 213
social illusion, cognitive bias as, 110
social justice movements, 144
social media
    celebrity worship and, 17–18
    and desire to be internet famous, 137
    morally judgmental women on, 144
    vlogs of cancer patients as healthy use of, 99–100
    wellness quacks and, 46
    and zero-sum bias, 79–81
    see also specific platforms, e.g.: Instagram
socioeconomic status, zero-sum bias and, 78
Sow, Aminatou, 88
spiders, cannibalism by, 27
"spiritual bypassing," 40–41
spontaneous trait transference, 83, 87–88
"Stan" (Eminem), 9
stans (celebrity worshipers), 9–11, 16, 18–27
    reactions to betrayal, 24–25
    and social media, 18
    Taylor Swift and, 10–11
    treatment of famous women by, 26
Station Eleven (Mandel), 182
storytelling, 159
    "but/therefore" vs. "and then," 103
    as technique for creating illusory truth, 155, 159
student loan debt, 102
subtractive solutions, 63–64

success
    success–failure binaries, 101
    zero-sum bias and, 78
sunk cost fallacy, 52–69
"Sunk Cost 'Fallacy' Is Not a Fallacy" (Doody), 59–60
superstition, 36
survival, halo effect and, 12
survivorship bias, 90–106
    defined, 90
    exclusion of invisible failures, 97
    Racheli's wariness of, 95–96
    WWII fighter plane armor study, 96–97
Svenson, Ola, 134*n*
Swift, Taylor
    and "Borderline-Pathological" category of standom, 23–24
    cult-like behavior of stans, 181
    and social media, 18
    stan scandals, 10–11
    stans' online reactions to criticism of, 20
    stans' reaction to Ticketmaster problems with 2023 tour, 20–21

T

Tales from Earthsea (Le Guin), 187
Tavris, Carol, 144, 174–175
Taylor, Jill Bolte, 165
technology
    combining with human inventiveness, 217
    and democratization of information, 158
    and overconfidence bias, 137–138
teenagers, *see* adolescents
television, nostalgia for recent eras on, 190–191
"tempusur," 201

INDEX

Thiel, Peter, 101
Think Like a Monk (Shetty), 38
Thomas, Leah, 199
Thunberg, Greta, 203
Ticketmaster, 20–21
TikTok
   astrology on, 179
   IKEA effect and, 210, 211
   and internet fame, 137
   self-misdiagnosing of mental disorders on, 32
   and social comparison, 85
   use disorder, 81–82
time
   brain's treatment of, 189–190
   human perception of, 122–126
"Tinder Swindler" (Simon Leviev), 131, 142
To Be Magnetic (self-help program), 37
Tobia, Jacob, 82
Together (Murthy), 87
tokenism, 82
Torres, Rachel, 134, 139–141, 147
toxic relationships
   cultlike aspects of, 67
   "love-bombing" in, 66
   societal factors that perpetuate, 62–63
   sunk cost fallacy and, 52–69
toxic stress, healthy social connection as antidote to, 87
tradwives, 187, 189
trait transference, spontaneous, 83, 87–88
trauma, conspiracy therapy and, 40, 44–45
tropes, 160
Trump, Donald
   and declinism, 194
   Norman Vincent Peale and, $39n$
   Taylor Swift and, 10
   see also presidential election of 2016
trust in American institutions, loss of, 16–17
Tumblr
   stan culture and, 18
   Taylor Swift and, 10–11
Tversky, Amos, $3n$
Tversky, Barbara, 162
Twitter
   IKEA effect and, 210–211
   morally judgmental women on, 144
   spread of true versus false stories on, 44
   Taylor Swift fans and, 20

U

Uddin, Shahamat, 141–142
Unidentified Aerial Phenomena (UAP/UFOs), 107–110, 112–14, 117–119, 125
Universe Has Your Back, The (Bernstein), 38
upward social comparisons, 81–82
urgent-vs.-important matrix, 121–122

V

vaccine-related misinformation, 41
venting, catharsis hypothesis and, 83
Vietnam War, 16
vlogging (video blogging)
   by cancer patients, 90–95, 99–106
   and line between real experience and storytelling, 103–104
Vulture magazine, 20

INDEX

W

Wagage, Suraji, 40
Watergate, 16
Waters, John, 203
wealth, survivorship bias and, 101–102
weddings in Middle Ages, myths about, 151–154
Weezer, 210–211
Weiner, Aaron, 31, 45–47
"welfare queen" trope, 160–161
Whalen, Sean, 41
Wheeler, McArthur, 129–130, 131, 138
"When Did We Start Taking Famous People Seriously?" (Grose), 16–17
When Genius Failed (Lowenstein), 135
white men, deaths of despair and, 196*n*
wilderness, 127
Wineland, Claire, 92, 93, 102, 103, 105, 106
Winfrey, Oprah, 37
Winnicott, Donald, 26
win-win denial, 75, 85–86
women
  and morality, 143
  and zero-sum bias, 81–82
Woolf, Virginia, 122
World War II, fighter plane armor study during, 96–97
"World Without Words" (*Radiolab* episode), 165
wytai, 195

Y

Year of Magical Thinking, The (Didion), 5
YouTube
  "New to You" category, 111*n*
  UFO videos on, 118–119
  vlogging by cancer patients, 90–95, 99–106
YK, 177–178

Z

Yuen, Eddie, 194–195
Zen Buddhism, 6
zero-sum bias, 73–89, 181
Zwicky, Arnold, 111

About the Author

AMANDA MONTELL is a writer and linguist from Baltimore. She is the author of the acclaimed books *Wordslut* and *Cultish*. Along with hosting the podcast *Sounds Like a Cult*, her writing has also appeared in *The New York Times*, *Harper's Bazaar*, *Marie Claire*, *Cosmopolitan*, and more. She holds a degree in linguistics from NYU and lives in Los Angeles with her partner, plants, and pets. Find her on Instagram @Amanda_Montell.